TEACHERS AND THE
NEW THEOLOGY

William Strawson

TEACHERS AND THE NEW THEOLOGY

LONDON
EPWORTH PRESS

Printed in 11/12 Baskerville
by Ebenezer Baylis and Son, Ltd,
The Trinity Press, Worcester, and London

SBN 7162 0124 0

Contents

Acknowledgements

Bible quotations are from the *Revised Standard Version*, Thomas Nelson and Sons Ltd, © 1965, and from the *New English Bible*, Oxford and Cambridge University Presses, © 1961, and are used by permission of the publishers. Acknowledgements are also due to John Farquharson Ltd for permission to include an extract from *A Kind of Loving* by Stan Barstow, and Constable & Co. Ltd for permission to quote from *Objections to Humanism* by H. J. Blackham.

Foreword

I can best explain the intention of this book by describing how it came to be written. A little time ago I was approached by the Institute of Education of the University of Birmingham on behalf of teachers of religion in schools who were concerned about the effects of new theology on their work. As one teacher put it, 'As soon as I have managed to read one of the latest paperbacks about some aspect of new theology, and think I am now up to date, a sixth-former comes along and says, "Have you read this new book by so and so, and what do you think of it?" Or some wag in the staff room remarks, "I suppose R.E. will be taken off the syllabus now that the theologians say that God is dead." '

This is a very understandable *cri de coeur*; for theological thinking is moving so fast that an ordinary working teacher can be excused for thinking that he can no longer be sure what to teach, and is ready to give up in despair. It sometimes looks as if new theology leaves us precious little to teach anyway.

What I have attempted in this book is not a short and easy answer to dangerous trends in modern theology. Indeed, I hope it will quickly appear that my purpose is much more constructive. I happen to think that we have a great deal to learn from contemporary developments in theology. I am most concerned to narrow the gap between theologians and teachers, because I believe that there is urgent necessity for teachers to base their approach on a tenable theological position, and not on views

which can only be accepted by doing violence to their intellectual integrity. Incidentally, as a practising theologian, I find it a
salutary exercise to attempt to interpret modern theological
thought in terms that can be useful to teachers, for unless our
theology is teachable, I think we must doubt whether it can be
true.

So this is a book about the content of religious teaching more
than about methods of using the material, although I have ven-
tured to give some suggestions about the way these ideas will
affect classroom work. And while I have particularly in mind
the teacher of more senior classes, I venture to suggest that this
should also concern every level of the school. For it cannot be
good that infants and juniors should be taught religion on the
basis of traditional belief, and then introduced to contemporary
ideas about religion at a later stage. It is far more preferable that
from the beginning the teaching should have a basis such that
the teacher himself can wholly accept; and in my view no age
is too young for children to be introduced to ideas of God and
man which can be retained all through adult life.

I wish also to emphasize that this is not meant to be an easy
alternative to the reading of contemporary theology. I have tried
to give some idea of what the modern thinkers are saying, and to
indicate the positive value of some of their ideas. My intention is
to offer some help to those who are aware that much new thinking is going on in theology, and want to use this in their teaching,
but who need some guidance through the complexities of this
steadily mounting literature.

I am grateful to the group of teachers who met at the
University and with whom I tried out many of these ideas.
Their practical experience has helped me to see the real problem
facing teachers of R.E. today. Conversations with teachers in
various parts of the country have confirmed the view that such
an introduction as this may serve a useful purpose; and I repeat
that the benefit is not least to me as a theologian, for it helps
considerably to clarify one's views when one has to present them
in a form which may help teachers of children to gain a grasp
of the riches of the Christian inheritance.

1 | *Introduction*

WE LIVE in a day of the troubling of the theological waters. The titles of popular books remind us of the disturbed and troubled situation of our time: *Honest to God, Religionless Christianity, God is no more, The Grave of God.* In this situation teachers of Religious Education face a particularly difficult task because not only is there doubt about the content of our teaching, but we also have to face cross-fire from opponents of R.E., who wonder whether we should be teaching it at all. Humanists and secularists are increasingly vociferous in their opposition to the teaching of Scripture and Christianity in a time when so many parents of our children no longer practise Christianity in any discernible form.

The question, therefore, is what should we teach in a situation of so much doubt and questioning? This is both a question of what we should teach for the good of the children, and also a question of what we can teach and still retain our own integrity. Our first need is for the right approach. We need to have sympathetic understanding of the strange and even outrageous ideas being expressed by new theologians. Our attitude to these new ideas must not be one of complete rejection, nor must we simply accept everything they say without criticism or question.

An interesting point to begin with is whether theology can ever be 'new'. It seems reasonable to talk about a new baby, a new hat, or a new car, but can theology ever be called 'new theology'? What about the faith once delivered to the saints?

What about the given-ness of the Christian faith and the fact
that to most people the unchangeability of the faith is one of its
chief attractions? When we begin to consider the situation we
are in, we can ask firstly: Why has this suddenly happened?
Why have we suddenly come face to face with this new theology?
In part the answer is that it is always happening. One of the
characteristics of religious life is that there is a continual criticism of past ideas, however orthodox and accepted they may be.
Isaiah, for instance, was saying something really very radical
when he said 'Bring no more vain offerings . . . Your new moons
and your appointed feasts my soul hates' (Isaiah 1: 13, 14).
Hosea was expressing equally radical ideas when he said 'God
says "I desire steadfast love and not sacrifice, the knowledge of
God, rather than burnt offerings" ' (Hosea 6: 6).

To the contemporaries of these prophets, the sacrifices that
were being criticized were the main features of religious
exercises. It must have sounded to these prophets' contemporaries very much as if they were saying, 'Religion is finished. God
is no longer interested in your religious practices.' On another
level Job's friends tried to argue with him along orthodox lines
about the inevitability of suffering following evil-doing; they
drew the conclusion that because Job was suffering he must
have been an evil-doer. The whole argument of the book of Job
is an answer—a radical answer—to this orthodox approach.
Job will not accept the traditional stereotyped answers; he
wants to know what the real answer from God is. In his own
way he was as radical as Isaiah and Hosea; his particular
emphasis was apologetic rather than liturgical. When we turn
to the New Testament we find the same principles even more
strongly expressed. Jesus advised people who were going to
offer their sacrifices: first be reconciled to your brother
(Matthew 5: 24). This must have sounded very much like
saying, 'Don't go to church until and unless you have come to
terms with your relationship with your fellow men.'

Or again, Paul. When Paul said 'Christ is the end of the Law'
it is very difficult for us to appreciate what he sounded to mean
to his contemporaries. Law was the religion of the people to
whom Paul belonged. It was a divinely given way of life; it was
something which was perhaps more religious than anything we
have ever known; and yet Paul came to the conclusion that to

be in Christ is to see the end of the Law as a way of religion, as a way of pleasing God. And this process, which is easily illustrated from the Bible, can also be illustrated throughout the history of the Church. It is not only Reformers, so-called, who have from time to time radically re-shaped the Church; throughout its life the Church has continually produced people who have criticized accepted ways, including accepted ways of worship and accepted ways of morality, and they have propounded what seemed at the time extremely revolutionary notions. What is happening now is really a continuation of a process which has been going on at least since the Old Testament times.

But we could still ask, why did it have to happen to us just now? Granted that these radical ideas do appear from time to time in the Church, is there any reason why they should appear in our time? In order to answer this question, I think we first have to consider the fact that external pressures are having their influence upon the life and thought of the Church. I will mention at the moment five of these *external influences*.

Firstly, *urbanization*. In the western world people live increasingly in towns and this is affecting not only the external form of their life but also their way of thinking and their way of behaving in a quite remarkable way. Harvey Cox, in *The Secular City*, draws attention to the way in which living in an urban environment has, for instance, radically changed people's attitude to friendships. In the old village situation one had very little choice of friends; it was a case of either having friends in the place where one lived or having no friends at all. This, no doubt, produced many advantages of a small, closely-knit community, but it was also an impoverishing factor in people's friendships. There was a very limited range of people with whom one could have close understanding. Now in urban life a new situation arises. Because of the close proximity of large numbers of people, and because of modern transport, we do not have to be friends with the people who live in the same street. We can choose our friends from a much wider area. We can decide on other bases than mere proximity who shall be the people with whom we spend our leisure time, our cultural interests, and so on. This means that we have to think in terms of two relationships; one is the relationship with our near neighbour, towards whom we should have an attitude of understanding and sympathy and readiness to help, which often, however, falls short of close friendship. To the people whom we choose as friends we can have a much closer relationship which is not wrongly described as love. It is wrong for the Church to suppose that cities are made up of large numbers of small village communities, and that the task of the Church is to create communities in streets and local areas. This may indeed be going right against the tendency of modern urban life.

Then again, there is the question of planning involved in urbanization. It is impossible for people to live cheek by jowl in large conurbations unless they accept a high degree of planning in the physical features of their lives, in health, in education, in police services, and so on. The question then arises, how does this planning affect the individual's freedom? The problem of individual activity and personal choice can become very serious in an urban situation; but it is quite wrong to suppose that the only word of the Christian Church is a word to individuals. Robert Adolfs, in *The Grave of God*, emphasizes that in the past Christianity has spent nearly all its time talking about the private sector of life. The public sector has been almost entirely neglected, so that Christianity becomes purely personal; the only word of the Church seems to be to the individual in his situation; often encouraging him to rebel against the necessary planning of an urban life. But, as Adolfs and others point out, there may very well be much more that the Christian Church should do in expressing the faith in terms of our public as well as our private life. Maybe Harvey Cox goes too far in implying that the modern city is not far away from the kingdom of heaven upon earth. He is, I think, not sufficiently critical of the problems of urban life; but there is no doubt that urbanization has radically altered man's attitude to life, to his responsibilities to his fellow men, and to his environment.

Secondly, *secularization*. This is a word which, as we shall see later, is very much favoured by the new theologians. It refers especially to the way in which life is no longer dominated by religious judgements and religious tests. We see the effect of this, for instance, in relation to religious tests for occupations, and we all—rightly, I think—welcome the fact that a certain attitude to religion is no longer a bar to any appointment in State or industry.

The religious domination of education in the past arose out of the pioneer work of religious people, and the contribution of religion to education ought not to be forgotten. But most of us, I think, would agree that it is a good thing that the modern State has now taken responsibility for education, health, welfare, and so on. Nowadays religious authority no longer dominates our activities, our learning and our leisure time. We live in a secular world, and we have to come to terms with this secular world.

Another aspect of secularization we have to recognize is that it is an illusion nowadays to talk about Christendom as if everybody were more or less a Christian, and as if all we have to do is to maintain a steady flow of people who understand a faith that is accepted, but not understood by all. The situation is far more open than that.

On the other side, secularization in some cases means that every aspect of religious authority has been questioned, and there are those who wish to get rid of every vestige of it. For instance, H. J. Blackham, in his book *Religion in a Modern Society*, while prepared to grant that there should be religious teaching by the Churches, clearly feels that there ought not to be any privileged place for teaching of Christianity in State schools.

The third aspect of modern life which is radically affecting our attitude to theology is *the widespread questioning of authority*. I have no need to remind teachers that this is a very real problem. It is especially manifest in connection with belief and conduct. For whatever else people are prepared to accept on authority, they are not prepared to accept directions about what they should believe and what they should do. Many of us know that even quite young children are now well used to questioning everything that is said, even by their teachers. There are many causes of this questioning of authority in the modern world; partly, I think, it is a reaction from the necessary planning of urban life to which I referred above. We accept that a great deal of our life must be planned for us, but we jealously retain our own choice over personal belief and conduct. But there are other reasons for this questioning of authority.

The social structure has changed so much that there are in communities today no people in positions of absolute leadership to whom everyone else looks for guidance and authority. In the past it was the parson, the schoolteacher, the doctor, the policeman, or any who might belong to the aristocracy. These were the people who were in authority, and their authority was very often unquestioned. This acceptance of authority was especially widespread when there was an economic factor involved. When the getting or retaining of a job depended upon accepting the authority of the squire, or someone else in the local community, it was necessary to accept authority in order to live. This is no longer—or rarely—the situation today.

Another factor in this breakdown of authority which is more recent, and perhaps more worthy, is the effect of modern educational methods. For quite a long time now we have been teaching children to think for themselves, to come to their own judgements, to decide matters which are within their own province to decide. This is surely a good educational practice, and it has produced very good results. One result, which is sometimes not so easy to accept, is that children will question everything *we* say; they will question authority, they will question what their teachers say to them—this is what we had hoped they would do. We have to admit that the questioning of authority is one of the results—I would say a good result—of modern educational practice. When sometimes the problems of authority become severe, we do need to remind ourselves that we really have brought this on ourselves. We cannot blame anyone else for it, and I hope we shall never try, because it is surely a good thing: it is a sign of growth towards maturity that everywhere nowadays authority is questioned. We do not need less questioning of authority; rather, in our time, we need more of it.

The next factor to be considered is *the influence of science*. When science is mentioned it is usually with reference to the physical sciences, and no doubt a great deal of the influence of science is due to the way that it has made itself a universal provider. Many of the good features of modern life have been provided by the application of scientific method to all spheres of life. This has undoubtedly affected the way we think in a quite remarkable fashion. A great number of people who have no pretension to being scientists have some idea of what is involved in scientific method. They know that it involves gathering information through observation and, having looked at it, trying to decide the hypothesis by which it might be explained; they know that it involves further testing of this hypothesis, and then the formation of a theory, and further testing of the theory until a law is arrived at which is more or less universally applicable and through which we can not only understand our environment, but within limits, manipulate it for our own purposes.

I think, in passing, reference ought to be made to the fact that there do seem to be signs of many teenagers now rebelling against the over-dominance of the physical sciences. This is the cause of the problem of vacant places in some science faculties in Universities while there is a very great over-demand for places in human sciences and arts subjects. But still, we live in a scientific age, and this has undoubtedly affected our way of thinking to a marked degree. People see that science works; it produces accurate results. The question which can so easily be asked nowadays is: why cannot the problems of human behaviour also be solved by scientific method? Can we not find a way of deciding what is good and then proceed to apply it in a scientific manner? This would mean that we should have an accurate assessment of what is required, and we should have a method which would work—for the scientific method, generally speaking, does work. All this seems to undermine any sort of relation between religious faith and morality.

Then again, the science of psychology still appears to many to be a substitute for religion. Instead of going to Church to get rid of our guilt feelings, the thing to do is to recognize that these guilt feelings arise out of a wrong understanding of our relationships with other people and with the world. If these guilt feelings become too marked, then the thing to do is to go to a psychiatrist who will talk to us and, if necessary, give us some treatment—and we shall get rid of our guilt. The psychiatrist in this way becomes the modern priest.

Another science which has in recent years become far more influential is sociology. Sociology, called by some people 'a humanist inquiry', apparently sets out to explain everything by reference to the choices people actually do make, and to the way in which they actually do react in certain situations. The question of how they ought to react, or what decisions they ought to have made, seems to be outside the realm of sociology. Confining the method to finding out what people actually *do* think and say and do can lead to a view of life based upon what actually *is* and not what *ought* to be. It is easily seen that this approach can readily imply that religious ideas are the result of our environment and our teaching, and that they do not necessarily have any objective truth in them at all. I think there is no doubt that quite a lot of popular sociology has seriously undermined confidence in the Christian faith.

Next we have to look briefly at the contribution to this modern situation made by *modern philosophy*. Here particularly, we have to notice the school of philosophy, very dominant in this country, which is usually called 'linguistic philosophy'. I am not arguing that many people are in fact linguistic philosophers. The vast majority of the population would not even look at a book of linguistic philosophy if they had the chance; but there is no doubt that linguistic philosophy has expressed in consistent form the attitude of many people to religious ideas. The main object of linguistic philosophy is the examination of the meaning of language. Philosophers of this school do not presume to be able to tell us much about great metaphysical questions— the meaning of life, and all that sort of thing. More reservedly, they attempt to examine statements which are made, and point out the meaning of these statements and sometimes their inconsistencies. Their attitude to religious statements, generally speaking, is very critical. This is largely because they think that statements about God look as if they were about a state of affairs, about matters of fact; but when the linguistic philosopher applies his test, a test which he calls 'verification', he points out that there is no means of knowing whether or not what is being said is true. For instance, if you say 'God is love', the linguistic philosopher asks how you verify or falsify this statement; that is, in what circumstances would you be prepared to say it is not true. The religious person usually responds by saying that whatever the circumstances he would still not say it is untrue because this is a matter of faith; there may be many external circumstances which seem to deny the love of God, but still he will maintain to the very last that God is love in spite of all appearances. Now, the linguistic philosopher says, this no doubt is very praiseworthy as an attitude of faith, but it is not

satisfactory from the point of view of the verification principle.
Religious statements which are true whatever happens, in every
circumstance whatsoever, have suffered death by a thousand
qualifications, as Antony Flew has reminded us. It is this
critical approach to religious language which often proves a
real stumbling block to people in their attitude to religion; they
cannot convince themselves that religion is about anything at
all to do with reality. Statements of religion are really unaccept-
able because they are not verifiable or falsifiable.

In addition to these external pressures we ought to notice that
there are some pressures which lie midway between internal and
external pressures, and are also assisting in this process of creating the need for a new theology. I have already mentioned the
effect of the end of religious authority in my discussions of
secularization and the questioning of authority. But a little more
ought to be said on this line.

In the nineteenth century you were either a Christian or an
atheist, and if you were an atheist, generally speaking, you were
regarded as a bad lot. Your morality was often questioned by
people who perhaps ought to have known better, and many
openings in public life were closed to you. The case of Bradlaugh,
the Northampton M.P., is a very good illustration of this: the
long struggle he had before he was able to take the Oath of
Allegiance as a Member of Parliament, and the eventual changing of the form of that Oath as a result of this particular case. I
think there is no doubt that, as a result of these pressures towards
religious conformity in the nineteenth century, there was a good
deal of submerged atheism and agnosticism masquerading as
orthodox Christianity. But this is not the case today. Nowadays
you can be an atheist openly, without any sort of inhibition or
limitation; indeed, it sometimes seems as if atheism, agnosticism, humanism and secularism are all more intellectually
respectable than Christianity. People now have a real opportunity to differ from religious conformity, and in many cases
they have grasped this opportunity with both hands. This raises
great questions for those who still maintain their Christian
faith.

In addition to this, the fact is that now as never before real
alternatives to being a Christian are possible to people in this

2

country. We have always known that there were other religions in the world; we knew that some people were Hindus, Buddhists, Moslems, and so on, but often our missionary enthusiasts gave the impression that people who had this sort of attitude to life, who embraced these non-Christian religions, were really very primitive people, and our task as Christians was to go and enlighten them, to bring them out of the darkness of their paganism into the clear light of Christianity. But now many of these aforesaid Hindus, Buddhists, Moslems etc., have come to live among us, and we have to admit that in many cases their religious practices are no more reprehensible than ours. They may be different, there may be many things that we can question in the attitude of non-Christians, but we surely can no longer delude ourselves into thinking that the only really respectable thing to be in the world is a Christian. So we have come face to face with the possibility of other religions; and even if we don't become an adherent of any of these non-Christian religions, there is no doubt that their very presence proves a real undermining of the absolute authority of Christianity. There is especially an undermining of the authority of a Christianity which claimed to have not only the truth, but the whole truth absolutely, which no one else was supposed to have at all. Now this situation has radically changed, and we are face-to-face with the possibility of real alternatives to being a Christian.

Christianity in this country is now a minority movement. Quite a lot of our Church structures and organizations have still not come to terms with this fact, but in terms of organized religion, public worship, and the influence of Christian bodies, this is so. This massive defection from organized religion has created a great crisis of confidence in the Churches. I think it is true, as modern writers are saying, that there is a great loss of confidence in worship—we often seem not to know what is happening, if anything. When we attend our places of worship, we often find that there is no Christian answer to the problems which modern life raises, and we have lost that old assurance about the reality of God and our relationship with him that our fathers used to have. In this situation it does look as if the best thing for Christians to be is, as John Robinson says, 'Honest to God'; at any rate Honest-to-God ignorance may be better than the appearance of comprehensive knowledge which is not based upon reality. No longer can a Christian say to his contemporaries 'I know the answers. You just ask the questions and I'll tell you what the answers are.' We find nowadays that our contemporaries no longer ask the questions to which we used to think we had the answers. The questions they ask are in many cases questions that we also want to ask, because we, as much as they, are in a position of questioning and conflict and doubt. This is the situation which radical theology has made us face in all its grim reality.

We now have to consider the *internal pressures* which have been building up in theology at the same time as this cultural and scientific development. The process of theology in the past fifty or sixty years can be shown to be inevitably tending towards the present situation which issues in new theology. There are several factors in the theological situation which have to be taken into account.

1. *The Bible*

Since the critical view of the Bible became widespread and well known, this has been very influential in all matters of faith, especially for Protestants, although it is also true that it has been taken seriously by Roman Catholics. In recent years, certainly, Roman Catholic theologians have given far more attention to the Bible, and as a result the questioning of the historicity and reliability of the Bible affects Roman Catholics almost as much as it affects Protestants. We all know that it is still possible to find people who do not accept the critical view of the Bible, to whom divine authorship is still a lively question, by whom theories of literal accuracy and literal inspiration are still taken seriously. But most people will agree, I think, that these questions really belong to the past. We are no longer much bothered about the literal accuracy of many of the historical parts of the Bible; the question of the relation between the scientific attitude and the story of creation in Genesis I is no longer a live issue for most of us. We realize that the Bible is speaking on a different level, answering different problems from those raised by science. Nevertheless, the problems continue to arise in connection with Bible study. I think one of the clearest features of the modern attitude to the Bible is the problem of its irrelevance to a large number of people. Those of us who are regularly attempting to teach Bible subjects know that again and again the real question is not 'Is this true?', or 'Did it happen like this?', or 'What does it mean?', but rather 'What has this to do with us at all?' It seems to have no relation to our ordinary life in any shape or form.

A good illustration of this is the way in which the recent publication for schools of the Shorter Revised Standard Version of the Bible has not met with anything like the same success as the series it replaced, which was a shorter version of the Authorized Version. The fact is, so the publishers believe, that in schools the Bible is no longer taken as seriously as it used to be. It is no longer a staple part of the cultural inheritance of children. This is a factor which also has to be taken into account in assessing the position regarding the 1944 Act. At present it is perhaps unfortunate that the foundation of the agreed sylla-buses connected with the 1944 Act was a biblical basis. One of the chief reasons for this, I fear, was not so much a very wide agreement about the central significance of the Bible, as the fact that the Churches thought this was the only basis on which they could reach agreement and be able to accept an agreed syllabus. So all our agreed syllabuses are based firmly and almost en-tirely upon biblical material. This happened at a time when already the significance and relevance of a great deal of the Bible was under question, and I think we are now faced with the problem of what we do about this large amount of biblical material which is undoubtedly very valuable for devo-tional purposes, but much of which can be questioned as to its usefulness in teaching religion to children.

In particular, I want to mention the way in which the critical attitude to the Bible has affected the study of the gospels. This indeed has become a central subject because, as we shall see, modern theology lays increasing emphasis upon the Person of Christ, and therefore the records of his life and teaching are bound to be of great significance in modern theology. There are two attitudes to the interpretation of the gospels that must be mentioned. One is Form Criticism and the other is Demytholo-gizing. Both these attitudes to gospel study owe a great deal to the work of Rudolf Bultmann, and it is significant that in both cases Bultmann came to his interest in these approaches through his concern for the communication of the Gospel in our time. When he was a chaplain in the First World War Bultmann came up against the problem of communicating Christian ideas to non-Christians, so that behind his interest in form criticism, and especially in demythologizing, there lies this deep concern for the communication of the Gospel. This needs to be kept clearly in mind because some of those who are now expounding new theology think that the communication of the Gospel to unbelievers is not a very significant part of the Church's task. They regard the Church's main task as making sure that those who believe in Christ do so in a secular way. They are not very concerned about evangelizing the secular world, but rather about secularizing the believing world. But at any rate, as far as Bultmann was concerned, this problem of communication was central to his thinking.

Form criticism is a not very happy translation of the German *Form geschichte*. The literal meaning of this phrase is form history. It means the history of literary forms found in the gospels. The approach of the form critics is based upon the belief that an investigation of the period prior to the written forms of the gospels reveals that they were originally constructed out of very small units of tradition which have been put together by editorial hands in order to demonstrate certain distinctive features of the theology and life of the early Church. The form critics do not assert that there is no historical material in the gospels at all. What they do say is that every part of the gospels comes to us through the mind and life of the early Church and, therefore, in order to understand the significance of the gospel traditions, we have to try to understand the situation of the early Church. Bultmann and, even more, Martin Dibelius, both assert that one of the chief activities of the early Church was preaching. They believe that we have therefore in the gospels, material which was used in the preaching message of the early Church. This means that the basic question that the form critic thinks should be applied to the gospels is not 'Is it historically accurate in every detail?' but rather 'What does it say about the person and work of Jesus Christ?' The problems raised by form criticism are especially connected

with the matter of the historicity of the gospels and the question
of whether we can know enough about the historical Jesus to be
able to identify the experience of the Christ of faith and link it
with the historic reality of the revelation in Jesus. There is no
doubt that this attitude has much difficulty for many people because they think that the form critics have taken away so much
of the historical reliability of the gospels that now there is not
enough left for a sound judgement to be made and for Jesus to be
identified.

On the other hand, the advantage of the form critical
approach must be recognized. This is especially in connection
with the realization that the Christian life is a life in Christ; it is
a life of living with a person who is alive now; the Christ of
faith is known in the life and worship and service of the Christian community. Form criticism has made it more possible for
twentieth-century Christians to see their unity with first-
century Christians. We no longer have to think of ourselves as
the followers of a dead hero whose wise words, spoken nearly
2,000 years ago, we must try to adapt to our own circumstances.
We realize that we are in the same position as the early Church.
Christ must be for us, as he was for them, a living reality in the
present, a reality confirmed and filled out and given content
through the tradition which is enshrined in the gospels. Only in
this way can we make the Christian faith relevant to our own
age. The historical question cannot be brushed aside as of no
significance, but we must continually recognize that the questions of meaning and faith are of greater importance than the
questions of historicity.

Demythologizing is another approach to understanding the
gospels, and also other parts of the Bible, which has been influential in our time. Most of us are, in fact, well used to the
process of demythologizing, but usually we do not call it by this
name. For instance, when we read in the Bible that 'The heavens
are telling the glory of God', or 'God dwells in heaven and
looks down upon the earth from heaven', we regard these expressions as symbolic terms which express a truth about God
in a way which was suitable for the time in which the expression
was used. We do not seriously think that to believe in Christ as
revealed in the Bible we have to believe that the heavens are
composed of a sort of upturned basin placed upon a flat earth,

and that in this basin various holes are made through which we see the light of the sun, the moon and the stars. We know that this first-century cosmology has been out of date ever since the time of Copernicus. We do, therefore, demythologize some of the terms of the Bible without any difficulty. We do the same, I suspect, regarding such terms as 'angels', and 'the end of the world'. Sometimes, of course, in failing to demythologize we can arouse greater difficulties than otherwise there would be. For instance, the phrase 'the clouds of heaven', which is often used in passages referring to the coming 'end of the world', can easily be taken as a reference to rain clouds. But in fact 'clouds of heaven' means the heavenly transport system—the way God and angels and spirits move about the world and come into human life. It really has nothing at all to do with any sort of clouds as we normally know them. So far, so good—we all to our own satisfaction demythologize. What Bultmann and other people have done is to apply this same principle on a much wider basis. For instance, what is the meaning of the titles of Jesus? Jesus referred to himself as 'Son of Man'; he was referred to as 'Messiah', and as 'Saviour'. Do these terms need demythologizing in our time? The method of demythologizing is first of all to understand what the term meant in its original use, then to try to find words which will make it possible to express the same idea in our context. Strictly speaking, it is not a matter of getting rid of myths but of finding suitable myths for our own time. The question which arises here is, what are the suitable myths, suitable expressions, that is, in which we can speak about the Person of Christ in our time? Some modern theologians have made considerable efforts to express the idea of Jesus as our contemporary; they want to use terms which are taken from our ordinary culture, such as shop steward, or president, or something similar, rather than words which belong to an outdated culture, such as 'Son of God', 'Redeemer', or 'Messiah', because these words really mean nothing at all to modern man. This process of demythologizing is sometimes disturbing because we like to hang on to the terms and expressions we have become accustomed to. Again, I think, as with form criticism, demythologizing does bring a great release from this bondage to outdated ideas which are no longer relevant to our time. We need to recognize, therefore, that in trying to understand the gospels and the whole Christian message we shall need continually to demythologize and then to remythologize in order to make the message understandable.

2. *Theological developments*

What has been happening in the field of systematic theology during the time when the critical view of the Bible has been developing? It is very difficult to know just where to start in this connection. Indeed, one could start anywhere and trace the development of doctrine from that point, if necessary even going right back to the beginning of the Church. But we have to break in somewhere, and therefore I choose to break in at the beginning of the present century. At that time the dominant theological emphasis was theological liberalism. This was especially centred on the idea of the Jesus of history; it involved an open rejection of dogma which was thought to obscure the reality and simplicity of Jesus. The Christian way was seen to be a way of following the simple teaching of Jesus, and all the so-called doctrinal complications of Paul were regarded as additions to the simple gospel and therefore to be ignored. In the same way there was a great belief in human progress; man was on the up and up, and was continually developing his latent powers. This, we must admit, was a very powerful approach to a simple Christian faith, and it had a great effect upon large numbers of people. There is no doubt that it made Jesus seem real, especially after the over-dogmatism of the previous period, but it did build up a dream world—a dream world of progress and potentiality, of inherent goodness, and so on. This dream world was shattered by two events which were very closely connected. One was the First World War. Suddenly it was realized that the idea of gradual and consistent progress did not fit the facts. The other 'event' was the advent of Karl Barth, who in the early days of the First World War recognized the moral ineffectiveness of this liberal Christianity. He found that the faith that he had been brought up to believe, connected as it was with an idealistic philosophy, was now quite useless to face the challenges and problems of the new situation brought about by world war. And so Barth developed his emphasis in what appeared at the beginning to be an entirely different direction. Instead of an emphasis on the goodness of man, he spoke of the sinfulness of man. Instead of the idea that the centre and totality of this religious devotion is Jesus, the simple Jesus, he placed the emphasis upon God as transcendent and wholly other. Certainly this God is revealed in Christ, but he is exclusively revealed in Christ; he can be found in no other way at all. The emphasis, therefore, falls upon the Word of God in revelation; confidence is placed in what God has done and can do, and not upon what man is or can be; upon the divine initiative and divine power, and the uniqueness of revelation. All this put a new strength and confidence into the Christian faith. This is undoubtedly demonstrated when we notice what happened in Germany under the Nazi regime. When the confessing Church really became effective in its opposition to Hitler, it was very largely expressing the views which it had learned from Karl Barth, and whatever we now see to be the disadvantages of the Barthian approach, we have to recognize it did prove itself effective in these most trying and testing circumstances. I personally would be very far from saying that the Barthian emphasis ought now to be forgotten or was unfortunate; I think it has made a very profound impact upon the theology of our time, and even if we are now developing from it, this is no argument against its validity and significance at the time. But there were difficulties, and these difficulties have become more apparent. One is the fact that there is a wide separation between knowledge of God discovered through divine revelation, and all other human knowledge. In his early period Barth was very antagonistic to philosophy. He did not believe that through the exercise of reason man could reach any certain knowledge of God. In fact he has modified this view in later years. The emphasis that many people find in his early teaching leads to a separation between theology and all other human knowledge. This is especially unfortunate because in this period that we are talking about there have been tremendous advances in all areas of human knowledge and human achievement, and the gap between theology and man's other knowledge has become wider and wider. It now seems to be so wide that there is no possibility of communication across it, and we begin to see that the mistake was to separate so rigidly knowledge of God from all other human knowledge.

The second difficulty of the Barthian position is to do with his attitude to man. As I have already mentioned, the emphasis was upon man as a sinner. Man is corrupt and unable by his own strength to find out any truth about God. This has had the unfortunate effect of producing in Christian teaching a sort of anti-human emphasis. It often sounds as if the Christian preacher and teacher is pushing man down; he is more concerned to point out man's faults than to recognize his potentiality; he seems to be against man; man is a bad lot and can only be put right by the intervention of divine grace. Now this attitude could, of course, be perfectly correct, although not very acceptable and not very popular. The question is, is it a right attitude? Is this true of man? When we look outside theology to the tremendous achievements of man in the past century, we are bound to ask, is it really true that man is such a bad lot? Can this man who has reduced infant and maternal mortality to almost vanishing point in this country, this man who is rebuilding his cities, who has tremendous hopes and possibilities for the future in spite of all the difficulties, can this man be such a bad lot? Even when full account is taken of contemporary problems and injustices—war, famine, racialism, man's inhumanity to man—it is still insisted that man must solve these problems, and is capable of doing so. And in any case, is the best way to help man to keep on pushing him down? Do we not need to see the positive side of human nature as well as its negative side? Another aspect of the same difficulty is that so often Christianity seems to be looking backwards to the Bible, to the early Church, to the Reformation, according to the particular ecclesiastical emphasis we may have. The simple fact is that this is not an attitude which is found in any other sphere to anything like the same extent. Modern man is not continually looking back; he looks forward. He has hope, he has ideas, he sees possibilities in the future. To keep on referring him back to something that happened a long time ago as if this is the only truth and there can be no further development from it is to present a very great stumbling block to modern man.

3. *Modern Prophets*

It is undoubtedly true that in this modern theological scene some people have had very great influence. I have already mentioned Bultmann and Dibelius; mention must also be made of Paul Tillich, the American theologian, whose special contribution to theology is along philosophical lines. Tillich's theology is what he calls an 'answer' theology, that is, we must first listen to what modern man's questions are and then we must try to find the Christian answers to them. This involves the acceptance of the fact that Christianity does not know all the right questions and all the right answers. Tillich's emphasis is philosophical in the sense that it is related particularly to a type of existentialism; he is continually seeking to relate Christian theology to modern culture and modern problems. Another name that should be mentioned is that of the German Dietrich Bonhoeffer who died as a martyr in a German prison, almost at the end of the last war. Bonhoeffer was a rebel against orthodox Christianity; he is recognized by many of the younger theologians of today as one of the great prophets of our time; some of the things he says are perhaps not so significant as they sound, but there is no doubt that Bonhoeffer's criticism of ecclesiastical authority and ecclesiastical structures, and his hesitation about the Barthian emphasis upon the depravity of man are very significant in the situation as it has now developed.

4. *The Problem of Suffering*
Turning away from academic theological pursuits, there are one or two things that ought to be mentioned which arise more within the context of ordinary people's religious experience. One of these is the intractable problem of suffering. It is true that there is an orthodox answer to the problem of suffering, and this is often some help. There is, for instance, the argument that there must be evil and suffering in the world consequent upon God's creation of man in freedom, and the assertion that again and again good comes out of suffering and God uses what appears to be something very terrible to effect good ends. These solutions are the common stock of religious apologetic, but to many people they have never been satisfactory. There is a certain rebelliousness which is not answered by these replies. Especially when we see those near and dear to us enduring suffering, we find the concept of a God who watches all this and has control over it, but doesn't really do anything to stop it, very difficult to accept. One of the ways in which modern

theology has tackled this is to question the assumptions of the
traditional theistic approach. Is it really true that we have to
think of God as apart from this world? Is he bound by the conditions of creating man in freedom and unable to do anything
about it? May it not be that if we look again at the concept of
God, and especially as we see him in Christ, we shall have a
different view? We may sometimes have to say that God does
experience failure. He is involved in our pain and suffering to a
far greater degree than traditional theism ever allowed. Connected with this problem of suffering are difficulties about
miracle and about prayer. Can we still believe in what is normally regarded as a miracle, which is supposed to be a divine
intervention into the natural order? Can we really believe in
this when we have a strong sense of the order and consistency of
the natural world? And if we can't believe in this, can we
believe in miracles at all? And is it true, as David Hume said
long ago, that Christianity cannot be believed without acceptance of miracle? This also comes very much into the sphere of
ordinary devotion because of the problem of intercessory prayer.
A great number of people who regularly go to church and
regularly say their prayers still wonder what, if anything, it is
supposed to do. Just what is the effect of interceding on behalf of
the people of Vietnam, or the coloured population of the
Southern States of America, or the friend or relative who is
dying of cancer? Does it really make any difference? These are
very practical problems which cry out for a better answer to the
question of the relationship of God with the natural world than
traditional theism has often produced.

5. *New Morality*

Another disturbing element in the modern religious situation is
the new attitude to morality. The background of our moral
teaching has often been that this is laid down in scripture as the
right way for humans to behave, and if we don't behave like this
a terrible effect will follow. There is, therefore, a continual
threat of doom of varying degrees if we do not accept the traditional morality. Now in our time many people have rejected the
traditional morality in all sorts of ways. The Church continually
seems to be fighting a rearguard action, slowly giving ground
when it has to, but undoubtedly giving ground all the time. The

simple fact is that if we look at the people who have rejected the traditional morality, it just isn't true to say that always they end up in despair, disillusion, sorrow and trouble. The new morality often seems to produce at least as happy an existence as the old morality ever could. The problem here is, do we still have to keep on fighting our rearguard action? Is this the proper province of a faith which ought to be leading mankind into a new understanding of its responsibilities and possibilities in this present age? You can't very well lead people forward if you are fighting a rearguard action. The question then arises, how can we break out of this defensive, defeatist sort of attitude regarding morality, and find something to say which would be helpful to people who in all conscience do need a lot of help with regard to the practical problems of life?

6. *Christian failure of nerve*

Without any question, organized Christianity has taken a terrible battering in the past fifty years. Measured in terms of church attendance, the Church has become a minority movement. This has resulted in considerable loss of confidence among people who still attend church and who are part of the organized Christian structure. This, of course, is inevitable. As soon as we become a minority movement we are bound to have to answer the questions of people who don't agree with us, and who want to know why we take certain attitudes and why we do certain things. The Church has also become extremely, maybe even pathologically, self-critical. We recognize that many of our ecclesiastical structures are now nothing more than a hindrance to a full Christian life. We find it impossible to accept many of the attitudes of traditional theism, especially on the metaphysical side, and we don't know what can replace these attitudes. We need, it is said, to get rid of the lumber which we have carried about with us too long. There are many things in the Christian luggage which ought to have been abandoned a long time ago, and because we haven't abandoned them, we present to people impossible demands in morality and philosophy and in an interpretation of history. So, the new theologians say, let's get rid of all that is not essential; let's go for the 'essence of Christianity', as one of them puts it. Let's discover what it really means to be a Christian. Even if we cannot answer all the questions, let's answer some of them in as realistic a way as we can.

The problem which this book sets out to answer is: when this stripping-down process is carried out (one cannot say when it is completed because it is never completed), when it is carried out, is there enough left? Is this reductionist Christianity worth keeping? Is there anything that the Church now wants to say, and is able to say, which is useful in the teaching and communication of the Christian faith generally? Or is it true, as some people are saying, that when this stripping down process is carried to its logical conclusion, there is nothing left; that the Christian faith has been evacuated of all meaning, and we might just as well pack up and say nothing, because we have nothing to say?

2 | *The Characteristics of the New Theology*

THE AIM of this chapter is to set out in as brief and clear a form as possible the characteristics of the new theology. When we have done this we shall be able to appreciate the contribution which has been made by the new theologians and we shall hope to be able to include in any new approach the insights gained from their work.

It is fortunate for our purpose that the new theologians are good at formulating slogans which often hit the headlines. These slogans can be used as pegs upon which to hang the outline of our summary of what the new theologians are now saying.

1. *God Is Dead*
This is one of the most remarkable and, some would say, shocking statements that new theology is making. It means different things to different writers. To some it means our language about God is meaningless, to others it means there is no such person as God. A few take it as the real meaning of the Incarnation. It is worth while asking what the grounds are for such a statement. In order to answer this question, I shall consider the work of three new theologians who all happen to be Americans. They vary considerably in their attitude to this idea that God is dead.

William Hamilton, in *The New Essence of Christianity* says that the characteristic of this new style of theology is willingness to listen; it is an end of the old claims to total knowledge. Theology has become diffident and ready to admit its own limitations. He argues that this humility is a proper attitude for theologians. We are now dealing with our own doubts and difficulties and not only answering the difficulties of the people outside the Church.

One reason for questioning the meaning of God is a very old one. It has always been understood in Christian theology that God cannot be objectified. He is not an object among other objects. He is unique, supreme—some would say, the supreme subject—but he is not to be objectified. St Augustine remarked that he only said anything about the nature of God in order to avoid a misleading silence. This reticence about the nature of God and the difficulty of making assertions about his nature has always been present with Christian thinkers, but in the past there has been a great tendency to cover them up, and external authority has often prevented these doubts from becoming articulate. But we now live in a time when there is no longer any inhibition to people expressing their doubts. The result of this is that the hidden doubts and problems which have always been present have now quite suddenly become open and acknow-ledged in the Church as well as outside it. These doubts have increased in number and strength because of the influence of the scientific attitude towards any claim to objectivity. Hamilton suggests that we have too readily accepted the scientific view that reality can only be known through sense experience. We have too easily accepted the view that unless an alleged existent can be verified empirically, it simply does not exist. One of the problems behind the 'God is dead' approach is whether it is based on a too ready acceptance of this logical theory, with the consequence that too much is given away. If Christian thinkers accept the principle that only that which is empirically verifiable is real, then inevitably we seem to have to accept the conclusion that God does not exist because God is not empiri-cally verified. We shall have to consider more fully the validity of this approach when we try to restate the Christian belief in God.

The second main contention of Hamilton is more closely connected with the views of ordinary people. This concerns the problem of suffering. Everyone knows that in the past Christians have given stereotyped answers to the problem of suffering. The problem is often expressed in the familiar form—either God cannot or will not prevent suffering. If he cannot prevent suffering he is not almighty; if he will not he is not completely good. So the fact of suffering, which is undeniable, denies either the omnipotence or the love of God. The traditional Christian replies to this difficulty run somewhat as follows: God has created man in freedom, and this necessarily entails that man must be able to do evil, and out of evil arises suffering. Antony Flew on several occasions has argued cogently that this 'free-will defence' of the Christian view of the goodness of God in the face of suffering is 'broken backed'. He claims that it is logically possible for God to have created man free to do only the good. There is no necessity of evil involved in the concept of freedom.

Other Christian defences in view of this problem of suffering argue that good comes out of evil, that even the most terrible happenings do produce good results, results which perhaps could not be produced by any other means. But the questioner is bound to wonder whether it is really necessary for all the suffering and cruelty to go on in the world in order to produce this supposed good. Could not God have so ordered things that there need not have been this terrible waste of human life, this misery and untold agony through which many people have to pass? The upshot of all this is that although many faithful Christians have come to terms with the problem of suffering, and indeed we often see the marvellous way in which sufferers are confirmed in their belief, yet it is true that attempted defences of the orthodox position have not been satisfactory. Hamilton suggests that what is needed is a re-examination of the theistic basis of this argument; that is, we have to ask whether the concept of a God outside the universe who is supreme and good is a satisfactory concept. Would it not be better to look upon God in a different light as one who is certainly more involved in the sufferings of mankind, maybe even involved in the failures of mankind? Hamilton suggests that only a God who can be thought of as defeated, only a God who is a failure, can really meet the problems of suffering humanity.

Hamilton goes on to remark that the experience of many people, especially in suffering, is that God is in any case remote and irrelevant. So this concept of the death of God has arisen. It does not necessarily mean atheism but 'a growing sense among non-Christians and Christians, that God has withdrawn, that he is absent, even that he is somehow dead.'[1]

While some regard this concept of the death of God as a very liberating one, it leaves many people in serious difficulties wondering just how they can come to terms with this new and frightening fact. Hamilton says a little later, 'For many of us who call ourselves Christians, believing in the time of "the death of God" means he is there when we do not want him in, ways we do not want him, and he is not there when we do want him.'[2] That is, we know about God in his absence and withdrawal as well as in his disturbing presence. This is probably a much healthier attitude than one which always looks upon the presence of God as a comforting and uplifting presence. Hamilton goes on to point out that in saying that God is dead but that he is now present in Jesus Christ, he is not to be understood as arguing that there is no knowledge of God apart from Christ, and he is not trying to rehabilitate a supernatural God under another name. He points out that the concept of the death of God does drive us to consider the significance of the Incarnation, but we do not come to Jesus, he says, because we can't find God anywhere else; we come to him because what we find about God elsewhere we can't accept or understand.

T. J. J. Altizer in *The Gospel of Christian Atheism* is more radical than Hamilton. In a very interesting and provocative way he uses the thought of the philosophers Nietzsche and Hegel to illustrate the way in which it is necessary for traditional Christianity to be broken down in order that man may be man. This seems to be one of Altizer's great principles. The reason why the transcendent creator must be removed from Christian thought is that the transcendent creator stultifies the possibility of man being fully human, and therefore it is necessary to assert the death of God in order to make possible the true life of man. Altizer suggests that one of the dangers of traditional Christianity is a backward look which is really an attempt to return to a primitive dependence upon an external and transcendent creator. As he says, 'A reborn and radical Christian faith must renounce every temptation to return to an original or primordial sacred, or to follow a backward path leading to an earlier and presumably purer form of the Word,

[1] Hamilton, *Op. Cit.*, p. 54.
[2] *Ibid.*, p. 63.

or to seek a total silence in which both Word and world will have disappeared.'[1] Many of the commonly accepted conceptions of Christian orthodoxy are regarded by Altizer as Christian inventions. For instance, the relationship between the guilt of man and the remoteness of God is a denial of the Incarnation. For in Jesus God has come near to men; indeed he lives in a human life. And there is remarkably little about guilt in the teaching of Jesus.

It is only when God is seen as far off and as separate from human life that man builds up this illusory sense of guilt. The radical answer to this denial of the Incarnation is an assertion that the Incarnation means that God is Jesus. God is Jesus means that God has died in order that he may become Jesus. To put the matter another way, the creator God has emptied himself to the point of denying himself in order that we may have the truth of God in Jesus. So instead of the remote God of theistic orthodoxy we see that the creator and redeemer are one. This, incidentally, means that when we come to consider the doctrine of the Atonement, we notice that modern theology no longer sees the problem in terms of the relation between a remote God and a sinful man, and Jesus as the mediator between the two; Jesus, who is God, is both creator and redeemer. This concept of God negating himself in order to be incarnate rests upon a view of truth which is based upon the thought of the philosopher Hegel. The Hegelian dialectic asserts that the advancement of truth is a process of internal self-development by means of contradictions. The well-known thesis-antithesis-synthesis process is an exposition of how reality is continually developing through internal clash and tension. The model used in the dialectical pattern is that of conversation. The thesis is the first statement that is made; the antithesis is the opposite of this statement; the synthesis is the new truth that arises out of the clash between thesis and antithesis. It is important to realize that synthesis is not compromise; it is essential to the dialectical conception that there is tension and clash between various ideas, and in this sense there is also negation; antithesis negates thesis. Now Altizer uses this to explain how it can be that God reveals himself by negating himself. The Christian name of God, according to Altizer, is the name of

[1] *Op. Cit.*, p. 40.

a process of absolute self-negation. This means that we have to think and speak of God in terms of dialectical process rather than in terms of substance. However much we object to this use of what seems a very remote and complicated philosophical theory to explain God, we have to admit that this at any rate is a breakaway from the old substantial idea which has dominated Christian orthodoxy for far too long.

Altizer applies this idea of the death of God, which he takes very seriously, in various interesting ways. He says, for instance, that in becoming present in Jesus the God who arouses a sense of dread and guilt is dead, so these concepts which are so significant in traditional religion must be largely abandoned. Then again, the Kingdom of God, according to Altizer, is not the continuing rule of a transcendent God, but the identification of the sacred and profane through the revelation and life of Jesus. All this is good news; Altizer is not speaking with his tongue in his cheek when he calls it 'the good news of Christian atheism'. He maintains that it is good news because it delivers man from the inhibitions of his former way of looking at things; it is good news because it tells us how God emptied himself and died in order that man may be in a new relationship with him. The thought of Altizer regarding the Atonement is very difficult to follow, but I think he means that salvation is effected through a change in God rather than a change in man; God at any rate shares in self-negation; he enters fully into the human situation and not only shares our lot but in fact shares our failure and defeat. Through this sharing man is given a completely new start, because there is a new view of God and a new relation to God, as seen in Jesus. Forgiveness of sins seems to Altizer the complete forgetting of sins; there is no question of any sort of payment or reformation that man must bring about; sins are removed by God forgetting them. In his affirmation of joy in the death of God Altizer is working with the concept of a stark either/or of transcendent/immanent. He thinks that it is not possible to have the combination of transcendent and immanent, which has been the normal attitude in Christian orthodoxy. Faced with these uncompromising alternatives he chooses the idea of an immanent God, and so completely abandons the idea of a transcendent God.

The third approach we can mention at this stage is Schubert

Ogden's. In his collection of essays, *The Reality of God*, Ogden makes it quite clear that he cannot be regarded as a 'God is dead' theologian. He does assert that God is the only issue worth considering in modern theology, and that the question theology has to face in our time is how God can be affirmed in what Ebeling calls 'the Age of Atheism'. The problem as Ogden sees it is particularly severe because this is an age which accepts scientific knowledge without question and in many cases not only says that scientific knowledge is valid, but that it is the only valid knowledge. Faced with this situation, Ogden says, some modern theologians have opted for the idea that God is dead. This certainly removes the difficulty of trying to speak about a non-empirical reality, but Ogden argues that it is tantamount to admitting that theology is no longer possible. In a very significant sense to say God is dead is theological nonsense.

The problem as Ogden sees it is that there are two concepts prevalent in modern society which conflict with each other; on the one hand there is secularism, which is the view that scientific knowledge is the only valid knowledge; on the other hand there is traditional metaphysical theism, which is directly opposed to secularism, because it affirms the reality of a transcendent being who cannot be known empirically. Now there are various ways of dealing with the tension between these two concepts; one can accept one concept and dismiss the other. This, Ogden asserts, is what the God is dead theologians have done. They have really opted for secularism. On the other hand one can choose traditional metaphysical theism and deny secularism. This is the attitude of the religious conservative. But there is another way out, says Ogden, which involves the denial of both these assertions, and this way he proceeds to take. He denies secularism because he says it has no sound philosophical basis. How can it ever be proved satisfactorily that there is no knowledge outside empirical knowledge? This is a self-contradiction which cannot be maintained. Traditional metaphysical theism is also self-contradictory, for it speaks of reality which is extra to total reality and this is a contradiction in terms: if God is real he must be part of reality included in the Universe, and in this sense he is not transcendent. Not only so, but traditional metaphysical theism, says Ogden, is irrelevant to the modern situation. This last point is very significant. A great number of people who are not very bothered about logical inconsistencies and could not follow an argument about the possibility of traditional metaphysical theism being a contradiction in terms, nevertheless do realize that the concept of God becomes less and less significant in ordinary life. This indeed is one of the reasons why what some people regard as an outrageous theological view steadily gains ground. It does, in fact, meet the thoughts and problems of a large number of people, including people who call themselves believers. They do not see how belief in this transcendent 'other' God really makes any difference.

The solution that Ogden suggests is not that we assert that God is dead, but that we do deny traditional metaphysical theism. This is not the same as denying God. It means that instead of thinking in spatial or substantial terms as traditional metaphysical theism always seems to do, we think in other terms. One way of putting it, says Ogden, is to say that theism means that we are convinced that life is worth while and trustworthy. He thus links ethics and religion very closely; both of them are on what he calls 'the boundary of explanation'. Ethics tell us what to do; religion enables us to put our hearts into it. This connection between ethics and theism could be very important in a modern understanding of what it means to believe in God.

If we consider an assertion such as 'this statement is true', or 'an attitude of love is basically valid', we are speaking in transcendental terms in one sense; we are speaking of something beyond, maybe above, human experience. We are not speaking in any sense in substantial or spatial terms. We can easily test this by noting that the questions 'where is truth?' or 'when is truth?' or 'how is love?' or 'what is the shape of love?' are really quite meaningless. And yet they do refer to something that is a very significant attitude to life. It may be that our modern conception of God will have to be more in terms of these ethical convictions than in terms of extra-spatial entities. A transcendent God need not be conceived in spatial or substantial terms.

We conclude that while the theologians who have been mentioned do say some very revolutionary things, and in some cases what appear to be outrageous things, they are nevertheless forcing us to consider the possibility that it is the framework of traditional belief in God which has to be broken up in order that a new framework may be constructed. Some people say that this is a wrong attitude, not only because the old framework has served so well in the past, but because if we try to construct a new framework we shall be equally on bondage to this before very long, and in any case it will not be a permanent solution. There are possible ways out of this difficulty. Many theologians and philosophers are saying that modern thought does not tend towards systems, therefore theology may not be tied to any particular system of thought, as once was the case. The answer to the point that we are not able to be sure that our solution will be permanent is that this is not our business; our business is to find a solution which will serve us in our time. We must be ready to admit that within a generation or two other ideas will have come along, perhaps to some extent built upon the ideas that we use, but it is no reason not to theologize because we cannot at the moment see how we can find permanent solutions. Some ways in which modern theology is speaking of God will be discussed in Chapter 6.

2. *The Secular*

This word is frequently used by modern theologians to express their attitude to the contemporary world. In order to understand the significance of their ideas we need to look a little into the background of the notions of the sacred and the profane. In Judaism one of the functions of the priest was to distinguish between the holy and the common (Ezekiel 44:23). The sacred is that which is separated from ordinary life and is not available for common use. This conception continues in various ecclesiastical ideas; tithes, priesthood, and church buildings are examples of things which are separated from common use by becoming sacred. This is not only an ancient attitude. Consider, for instance, the words used in the Service of Consecration of a Church in the Church of Scotland—'I do now declare this house to be for ever set apart from all profane and common uses and consecrate it to the worship and service of Almighty God.'[1] The same principle is expressed in the bread and wine of Holy Communion being 'consecrated'; that is, separated,

[1] *Book of Common Order*, p. 212.

withdrawn from common use, and set aside for a specific purpose in this service. Whether or not transubstantiation is accepted, this idea of that which is consecrated to God being withdrawn from common use still applies.

This relation between the sacred and the profane inevitably creates a dichotomy in people's view of life. Another inevitable result is that ordinary man fears the encroachment of the sacred upon that which is supposed to be for his own use. In order to prevent this encroachment man seeks to keep to himself objects of which he can say 'this is mine'. So life is divided into that which belongs to God and that which belongs to me, and I try to make sure that that which belongs to me I control and use according to my own desires. The difficulty about this is that it leads straight into the idea that religion is not about the whole of life, but only about particular sacred things and activities. This leaves a large part of human life without any influence from religion. Because of this dichotomy, until recently theologians tended to stress the unity of all life under the idea of the sacred. The dichotomy was criticized as false because, as it was said, 'all life is sacred'. There is no part of life which is not in some way affected by the idea of religion, and no part of life which is not under the influence of the will and purpose of God. One consequence of this idea is the notion that all things are sacramental, which seems a reasonable conclusion in view of the statement that all life is sacred. This led to considerable difficulties about the meaning of the gospel sacraments, for if all life is sacramental, why do we need any specific sacramental acts?

The new situation is that modern theologians emphasize the unity of the whole of life in terms of secularity rather than in terms of sacredness. They still insist that man must not divide life into two parts, but they point out that it is a mistake to regard the secular as of secondary importance and as being entirely dominated by the sacred. Modern theology has re-asserted the importance of ordinary things under the idea of the significance of the secular. That is, all life is secular.

In *The Secular City* Harvey Cox claims that our modern world has seen the end of religious and metaphysical control over the ordinary affairs of life. This is partly what is meant by secularity. Involved also in this is the conclusion that man is left in control of the world. As Cox puts it, 'The discovery by man that he has been left with the world on his hands.'[1] It will help our understanding of this subject if we distinguish between 'secularism' and 'secularization' at this point. Secularism is the attitude which makes an ideology out of the non-religious attitude. Sometimes it does this by asserting that scientific knowledge is the only valid sort of knowledge. Distinguished from this secularism is secularization, which Cox and others assert is a proper and inevitable development of biblical concepts. They point out that the Hebrews never despised the world; and they see in the modern freeing of education and politics from Church control a natural and good development of this biblical concept of the meaning of life.

One way of illustrating this point is to consider what Cox means by the 'desacralization of politics'. By this he means the separation of the ecclesiastical authority from the political authority. A good example of this in the Old Testament is the story of Samuel. Samuel represented the combination of the prophetic and political head of the nation. We read in I Samuel 8 of the complaint of the people. The goings on of Samuel's sons influenced them to refuse to continue under the same regime as had operated with Samuel. They wanted a king of their own, like other nations. Samuel was very distressed about this and he reported it to God in the prophetic fashion. God's answer was that the people would be allowed to have their king, but Samuel must tell them what the consequences would be. He must remind them that their taxes would be heavy and the demand of the king for slave labour and for chariots and horses would sometimes be very great indeed. There is, of course, another version of the same series of events a little later in the same book in which it is represented as according to the will of God from the first that a king should be appointed over the people of Israel. We need not at this point enter into a discussion as to which of these two accounts can be regarded as the more original. It is sufficient to say that in this separation of the political from the religious authority there was, in fact, a good development in the story of the Israelite people. If for a moment we think about the sort of kings who ruled over the Israelites, we can see how necessary it was that there should be

[1] *Op. Cit.*, (Revised Edition, Pelican, 1968), p. 16.

some check or balance to restrain the extreme wickedness of such kings and to bring the people back into the ways of truth and obedience to the will of God. It is very doubtful indeed whether prophet-kings would have escaped this tendency to be less worthy than they ought to have been, and without the attitude of the prophets there is no doubt that the story of Israel would have been very different from what in fact it turned out to be. So it does look as if the separation of the sacred and the secular in politics is a very good thing.

Cox goes on to speak of the characteristics of the life of the 'Secular City'. He says that the typical attitude of modern man is 'pragmatic and profane'. That is, truth is something to be done. The truth of any statement is to be found in the test of its effectiveness. Metaphysical questions are no longer interesting to modern man. He finds truth in profane ways of thought, that is, outside the temple. 'Urban secular man came to town after the funeral for the religious world view had been held. He feels no sense of deprivation and has no interest in mourning.'[1] As Albert Camus says, modern man finds the idea of God an obstacle to his own freedom and responsibility.

It is interesting to see this also from the point of view of a humanist. H. J. Blackham in *Religion in a Modern Society* claims that the religious domination of the State, which was a very bad thing, was caused mainly by the absolute claims of Christianity. He points out that quite often the modern secular state has advanced in spite of the opposition of the Church. He recognizes that some, like Hegel, see the secularization of religion as its proper development and he is certainly appreciative of the liberal solution which is found, for instance, in America. He quotes the view of Jefferson in 1785: 'Our Civil Rights have no dependence on our religious opinions.' This separation of religion and politics explains features of the educational scene in America which otherwise are very strange to us. The rigid separation of religion from politics means that there is no religious teaching as such in State schools. This has produced a very highly developed system of Christian education in the Churches and it is debatable whether our own way of bringing together State education and religious instruction has been more fruitful in its effects than the American separation.

[1] *Ibid.*, p. 93.

There is a further interesting illustration of the advantage of separating religion and politics in some of the views of Dietrich Bonhoeffer. Part of Bonhoeffer's important contribution to the subject of modern religion arises in his discussions with other leaders of the Churches which led to the formation of the German Confessional Church. Bonhoeffer asserted that a Church must be free to criticize the State. This indeed was one of the features of paramount importance in the German Confessional Church. He saw that a Church too closely allied with a political power is in no position to criticize that power. This was the inherent defect of the so-called German Christians. We ought to notice that at the same time Bonhoeffer was fully aware of the danger in separating completely Church and State. The State might become completely secular and have no place at all for the influence of Christianity.

Returning to Blackham's discussion, it is interesting to notice that he is quite sympathetic towards religious education in State schools. His comment upon the present situation is that religious education must not assume that the school is a denominational community. He seems much more in favour of a moral rather than a religious basis of education, and he rightly reminds us that Christianity has, as he puts it, 'no monopoly of high seriousness'. In the open-ended society, which he thinks modern society ought to be, there certainly should be a place for the practice and propagation of religious ideas but, Blackham argues, the proper place for these activities is the home and the community of Christians, not the school.

A book which investigates more thoroughly the relationship between the secular and the sacred is *God's Grace in History* by Charles Davis. Davis says that the secular is that which lies within the grasp of man's understanding, over which, because of his understanding, man has control, and that this area of understanding and control is continually being extended. The secular is, therefore, the area of immediate reality. On the other hand the sacred is the area of higher and deeper reality. The sacred is not even in principle knowable through human reason. It can only be known through the exercise of faith.

Now secularization, which Davis welcomes, is the extension of the area of the secular, that is, the extension of the area of that which is knowable, not necessarily that which is now known.

Some regard this extension of the area of the secular as a gradual and ultimately final elimination of the area of the sacred, but Davis sees this process rather as leading to a clearer delineation of the sacred. 'Christianity unites the secular and the sacred in a unity of order but it refuses to identify them.'[1]

Davis argues that secularization is indeed an advantage to the Christian faith. He speaks of 'the intrinsic compatability of secular culture with the Christian faith'.[2] This means that modern man does not have to make the unenviable choice of being either a Christian or a modern man, for according to Davis, it is possible to be both. Secularization is agreeable with the main assertions of the Christian faith rather than against them. For instance, the Christian doctrine of creation asserts that nature is not God, but it is dependent upon God; it is not to be worshipped, but it is to be accepted as a reality. This acceptance of nature as a reality which can be known and controlled is the basic assertion of secularization, and Davis argues that there is no contradiction here with the Christian doctrine of creation; rather, indeed, this is a proper working out of that doctrine. Similarly, the Christian doctrine of man made in the image of God implies that to man has been given authority and responsibility for the natural order. This is precisely what modern theology is talking about when it asserts that man has come of age. He is no longer dependent on any power outside himself for his use of the world in which he lives. God has given the world to man to be used. This means that any relic of the idea that part of nature is sacred and not to be known by man is contrary to the natural development of the Christian doctrine of creation and man. For instance, one sometimes hears Christians nowadays strongly asserting that whatever science can do it will never be able to discover 'the secret of life'. This seems to imply that we shall never understand how life began, nor shall we ever be able to produce living things from inorganic substances. That is, it is being claimed that this secret belongs to the sacred rather than to the secular. But surely the answer to this is that it is within man's power not only to understand life but ultimately to produce and control it, and unless we are prepared to limit man's responsibility in the sphere of the secular, we are bound

[1] *Op. Cit.*, p. 17.
[2] *Ibid.*, p. 20.

to say that we must not look for a relic of the sacred in nature in this way.

Davis goes on to discuss the significance of the sacred, and it is in this part of his discussions that the most valuable contribution is found. The sacred involves what he calls 'the mysterious transcendent' which man cannot locate. It finds man, he does not find it. 'Although God comes within the range of human knowledge he escapes man's understanding.'[1] This mysterious transcendent communicates itself through Christ and the whole sacred history. It is known by faith, not by reason, and indeed, when interpreted by reason alone, revelation tends to become secular and not properly understood. So there is a permanent element of the sacred in human life. It would be suitable to call this element of the sacred the supernatural, except that in popular thought this term has spatial implications which are confusing. Davis says that supernatural means 'what exceeds the proportion of nature'.[2] The implication of this remark is that there are various levels of reality, and the proportion of one is not the same as the proportion of the other. Particularly, grace is proportionate to the nature of God; so that the idea of the supernatural as Davis uses it means that there are various levels of reality. Here he is speaking of a level of reality which exceeds that which belongs to the natural order, but he is not in any sense speaking in spatial terms.

Davis makes a useful distinction between 'consecrate' and 'sanctify'. The consecration, or sacralization, of the world is the attempt to place everything under religious domination. This involves not only the reservation of certain aspects of life to the sphere of 'religion'—i.e. this area cannot be comprehended by reason—but also involves the idea that certain things can be withdrawn from common use, and this is what is meant by consecrating them. Admittedly there are proper elements of withdrawal in our relation to the world—the institutional Church is in a sense withdrawn from the world. But only so that through its life the sacred may be made manifest in the world.

To sanctify the world means not to withdraw from common use, but to make holy. That is, to understand and use ordinary

[1] *Ibid.*, p. 39.
[2] *Ibid.*, p. 43.

things in a truly religious way is to see them as part of total reality which has sacred as well as secular elements. So we must seek to sanctify the secular, that is 'to bring it (the secular) within a higher order, while retaining its consistency, value and function'.[1] We are not to look for the restoration of a 'sacred' or 'consecrated' society. We are to recognize the inevitability of the pluralist society, and we must live out our Christian faith in this society, without hankering for the return of former days of religious domination.

The value of Davis's analysis is twofold. Religious people are to welcome every advance in secular knowledge, every improvement in ordinary human affairs; and indeed to see these as the work of God. The non-religious man is to be encouraged to recognize that the secular world necessarily implies the reality of the sacred; the element in life which challenges man to high endeavour, and gives sense to secularity.

3. *Religionless Christianity*

Dietrich Bonhoeffer first used this phrase in a letter to a friend while he was in prison. He was asking a lot of questions about the future of the Church. 'What is Christianity,' he inquired. 'What is Christ for us today?' 'If religion is disappearing, will Christianity disappear with it?' 'If religion is no more than a garment for Christianity, then what is religionless Christianity?'

In order to understand the attitude of Bonhoeffer it is necessary to recall his great interest in the Church throughout his whole career as a theologian. In 1927 Bonhoeffer offered for his doctoral thesis a work on the Communion of Saints. In this work he writes: 'Communion with God exists only through Christ, but Christ is present only in his church, hence there is communion with God only in the church.'[2] The conclusion of his long study of the Church is that he sees the Church as Christ in the world. He is not in favour of the idea of no Church; his view is that the Church must exist for humanity. The Church must take part in social life, not lording it over man, but helping and serving man. The Church must tell man and show him that the fully human life is life for others, which involves rebuking in herself and in others pride, power, worship, envy, and humbug. The Church

[1] *Ibid.*, p. 54.
[2] *Sanctorum Communio*, p. 116.

must set before everyone, by word and especially by example, the value of moderation, purity, confidence, loyalty, steadfastness, patience, discipline, humility, content and modesty.[1]

So Bonhoeffer was contending for an alternative form of the Church. He was certainly not contending for the idea of the non-Church. But the alternative form of the Church would be, he thought, a Church which has got rid of all its endowments, and expresses its care for the poor in practical ways. The clergy would be maintained by free-will offerings of the Church and by their own secular work. The Church would be a servant, and as a servant she would not adorn herself with splendid buildings, with a superior position in society, nor claim for herself a high status. Everything about a Church must make it possible for her to be a servant. In his dispute with the German Christians in 1936 Bonhoeffer asserted that the nature of the true Church demands this concept of servanthood, and he claimed that the Confessional Church met this specification.

It is understandable, in view of the ideas outlined above, that some strong radicals believe that the whole ecclesiastical set-up is an obstacle to the servant mission of the Church. They say that it is not fitting for a servant to have such splendour and importance, even though it is now a very faded splendour and an almost-forgotten importance. A property-owning servant easily becomes too independent and disobedient. Too much energy is devoted to maintaining private property which not only takes up too much time and money, but also insulates the Church against the pressures of society. The Church still tends to live in a past age, vainly wishing for that age to return and refusing to come to terms with the situation as it now is. The problem, of course, is especially severe in the case of the Established Churches, but is also found amongst the Free Churches. For in all organized Christian communities bureaucracy, property and legal entanglements soon become obstacles to the true mission of the Church in our age.

The realists among modern thinkers recognize that it is in fact impossible to do what the hard radical recommends—to scrap the whole ecclesiastical machinery. As John Robinson says, we have to start where we are; we have to recognize that only by a process of wastage and renewal can the Church

[1] *Letters and Papers from Prison*, p. 166.

become what it ought to be. This does not mean indifference to the needs of reform. It means that every decision about Church extension or alteration of existing machinery, or about the question of which meetings should be continued and which abandoned, or what sort of services the church should hold— all these questions must be considered afresh in the light of the new situation which now faces the Church. Only by rigorous application of these principles to the developing life of the Church is there any hope that the Church will be renewed to carry out its divinely appointed mission.

All this can be extremely relevant to the situation of religious education in schools. To take first the question of secularity. Any teacher in any school knows that he or she is working in a secular situation. Indeed to some extent this is what creates the secular situation. It is modern education, especially with its scientific basis, which is producing the modern secular world, and no teacher of religion ought to try to avoid the implications of the secular world in which his work is to be carried on. The question of the relation between this secular world of the school and R.E. brings to the fore the problems of the relation between the sacred and the secular. Is R.E. the last coping stone that we add to the fine edifice of modern education? Is it bearing witness to the fact that there is something which is to be added to life which we usually call 'God', without which life is unfulfilled? Is it even, as some people think, to be regarded as a necessary counterweight to the advancing ideas of science and modern technology? It seems to me that in the schools is a wonderful opportunity for this extremely difficult problem to be seen and to be worked out. R.E. must not be a peripheral subject, bearing no relation to all the other subjects being taught. It must not be a subject on its own in a closed compartment of special interest to the pious among the children or the staff. R.E. must be involved in the total life of the school and must not in any way appear to be in opposition to the other things the school is teaching. In this sense the secular/sacred issue arises significantly in the school.

In a similar way the problem of religionless Christianity is relevant to the school situation. More than we realize R.E. has been based upon an assumption of a 'Christian' country. We still presume to think that all the children to whom we teach religion will eventually find their place in the life of the organized Churches, although a moment's thought will soon disabuse us of any such idea. Only a very small proportion of the children whom we teach are likely to belong to any discernible Christian community. This may mean that if we connect R.E. in schools too closely with the Church as it is now organized, we may be putting a millstone around our own necks. It may be better for R.E. to proceed independently of organized religion, for if we tie ourselves to organized religion we may be tying ourselves to something which has no future. On the other hand, a very strong case can be made out for the need for closer co-operation between Church and school to the benefit of both. It may very well be that many clergy and ministers will see the true situation in our secular society more clearly in the life of a school than they will in the life of their own regular congregation. It may be that in this way the school has a lot to contribute to the life of the Church; and the Church has no doubt a lot to contribute to the life of the school. I do not refer to the religious life of the school only. I would insist that the Church has a lot to contribute to the *total* life of the school. It would be very unfortunate if the Church gave the impression that it was only interested in the 'spiritual' side of modern education. This would be to deny the truth of Christianity. It is to the whole of man that the Christian gospel comes, and it is in the whole of human life that the Christian life can be lived. So that in the present situation there does seem to be a great need for a developed conception of the relationship between Church and school. We must not be unwilling to hear criticisms from each other. Both Church and school must be ready to see that we have much to contribute to each other's understanding of the present situation.

But the real crunch comes when we ask about the relevance of the 'God is dead' theology to the school situation. As we have seen, this phrase means various things, not all of them inimical to orthodox religion. But whatever the meaning of the phrase, it inevitably raises questions which go to the very heart of the religious education situation. Assuming that we are not prepared to give up in despair, the idea is a critical challenge to our subject. It raises in particular questions of meaning and relevance; both perhaps pointing the way to a better

4

understanding of the rôle of the religious educator. If the aim of all
education is to arouse an attitude of interest in one's surround-
ings, this will include asking about the meaning of common
words. What is the meaning of God? Here is a question which
will tax the resources of the most advanced thinker; yet at the
same time, a question which can be meaningful to every stage
of understanding. At least part of the function of the teacher is
to help his pupils to appreciate the meaning of the word 'God'.
This requires the removing of a lot of superstitious and wholly
inadequate ideas of God as 'up in the sky', 'a magnified father-
figure', 'an awe-inspiring judge, who is only concerned with
noticing our faults'. It would certainly appear to be necessary
for the teacher to have thought deeply about God before he
tries to interpret the notion of the divine to any group of
children.

But even when we have some idea of the meaning of God, we
do not necessarily have any idea of his relevance. So the job of
the teacher is to show that God, as understood in Christian
thought, is not someone to be 'accepted' and then forgotten.
Unless indeed God is seen to be closely related to the ordinary
business of life, it is doubtful if clear ideas about him are of any
great value. This is another way of saying that the aim of
religious education is not only to clarify the idea of God, but
also to show how God is to be known and experienced in life.
This experience is not to be thought of as a purely personal
and inward awareness of spiritual values, although I think this
meaning of religious experience cannot be entirely neglected.
But experience of God is also, and perhaps chiefly, an attitude
to the totality of life; believing in God is both seeing the significance of the sacred and committing oneself to a way of life which
arises out of conviction about the meaning and value of life. We
have to learn from the 'God is dead' theologians that there is an
aspect of faith which is not totally comprehended in terms of
the 'Other', for it also involves a commitment to a way of life.
If these theologians seem to be emphasizing the latter rather
than the former, it is because for too long the emphasis has been
in the other direction. Belief in God is as much concerned with
commitment to a way of living as it is to a conception of the
nature of things.

3 | *New Theology and Humanism*

WHEN John Robinson wrote his famous article in the *Observer*, entitled 'Our Image of God Must Go', a considerable amount of correspondence was evoked. Among the comments made were some by several writers of a humanist point of view who said that Robinson had indeed made a great contribution to the subject of God. Their main criticism was that his humanism had not gone far enough. Robinson himself says in *Honest to God* that often when listening to discussions between Humanists and Christians on the radio, or on television, he has found himself more in sympathy with the Humanists than with the Christians. All this suggests that there is at any rate a close similarity between new theology and Humanism. It is possible to illustrate this likeness by comparing various attitudes of new theology and Humanism, and noticing how close they are to each other.

'God is dead,' say some new theologians. 'There is no supernatural,' say the Humanists. New theology lays great emphasis upon the significance and importance of human life and the necessity of considering the fulfilment of life; it is mainly an emphasis upon this present life. Similarly, the Humanists often use as one of their slogans 'this life is all, and it is enough'. Or take again the attitude toward morality. New theology is very much inclined to agree with a 'situation ethic' which abandons most rules, certainly those which have a dogmatic basis, and argues that the essence of Christian morality is an attitude of love which must be expressed according to particular circumstances. It isn't a very big step from this attitude to that of the Humanist, who says that ethics is an evolutionary concept, that morality must continually develop according to the changing circumstances of people's lives, and that especially there must be no religious dogmatic basis for moral assertions. Indeed, some Humanists like Margaret Knight go so far as to say that the close relationship between supernatural religion and moral teaching is dangerous for children. The inevitable outcome of being taught about the supernatural, Mrs Knight thinks, is that eventually the child rejects this idea. If the child has imbibed notions of morality along with notions of supernatural religion, when the religion is abandoned the morality may also be abandoned. To take one other example of the likeness between new theology and Humanism; we have already noticed that new theology is an attitude of theological reductionism. It affirms that very often we have to strip down the Christian faith and leave aside unnecessary assertions until we reach a point where they can be made with certainty. We realize that consequently the whole spectrum of theological statements will not be covered. In a very similar way, Humanists often speak of uncertainty about God; they seem to have extended the range of reductionism to include the concept of God, and as we have seen, there are some theologians in our time who seem to be saying precisely the same thing. Certainly for an ordinary reader or hearer 'God is dead', and 'there is no God', seem to be synonymous. The Humanist will take us a step further in his attitude to the idea of the supernatural. Having pointed out the total uncertainty of any ground for belief in God, he often goes on to say that this in any case is an irrelevant matter. What we have to do is to get on with the business of dealing with problems as they arise. So it is often true that Humanists will not for long talk about any sort of metaphysical basis of their beliefs. They are much happier talking about moral problems like Abortion Law Reform, the necessity of peace throughout the world, the possibility of the reform of the penal system, and so on.

In view of these similarities it seems especially necessary in the present situation to consider the relationship between new theology and Humanism. In the past Humanism has largely been in encounter with old orthodox theology. Indeed the

Humanists often seem to prefer this encounter. If there is any suggestion that new theological concepts ought to be considered, they are apt to complain that they cannot well argue with so fluid a situation as modern Christianity sometimes presents. In other words, they much prefer a sitting target to a moving one! However much sympathy we may have with them in this situation, it is surely necessary that Humanism comes to grips with the contemporary exposition of the Christian faith, not with concepts and ideas which many Christians have already abandoned. With this in mind, therefore, we ought to consider now what Humanism is really about.

We have already given an outline of the attitude of the new theology, and in order to clarify the meaning of the encounter between new theology and Humanism we need to be clear about what the Humanist attitude is. This is all the more necessary because the word 'Humanism' is used in many different contexts, and indeed it is sometimes extremely difficult to know what is the precise meaning of the word. The situation is not made any easier by the fact that in the past it was reasonable to talk about Christian Humanism. For instance, the great scholar Erasmus is rightly described as a Christian Humanist, the reason for this being that he was both a very fervent Christian believer and also a very great advocate of new learning. He applied classical study to the study of the origins of Christianity and since, after the Renaissance, Humanism meant classical study, Erasmus was a Christian Humanist. There is no doubt that Christianity has learned and is still learning a great deal from the Humanist attitude, but in view of the declared convictions of those who now call themselves Humanists, which I shall shortly outline, it seems impossible any longer to use the term 'Christian Humanist'. If a Humanist is a person who does not believe in God, and who regards the Church as an obstacle to human progress, it seems difficult to understand how anyone can be a Christian Humanist.

In order to state objectively what the Humanist position is, I want to refer to the book H. J. Blackham edited, called *Objections to Humanism*, which was published in response to a challenge by a reviewer of an earlier volume called *Objections to Christian Belief*. In the later book Blackham writes an introductory article on 'What is Humanism?', setting out in a way which is not all that common among Humanists what the basic Humanist position is.

He begins by saying that Humanism stands for free inquiry; it is essentially anti-dogmatic; it involves a disciplined study of that which can be studied by human reason, and this involves the conviction that many so-called 'ultimate' questions are unanswerable. By 'ultimate' questions he means such questions as 'What is the meaning of ultimate reality?', or 'What is the purpose of life?' For these questions we simply do not have the apparatus to provide an answer. It is irrelevant to ask questions which cannot be answered. As I have already pointed out a Humanist soon begins to talk about social problems and ethical judgements, and Blackham is no exception to this. When he considers the question of the basis for morality he says morality is about conventions and procedures of human behaviour, and the basis for decision in these matters is social agreement. This does not require that everyone accepts exactly the same basis for their judgements, but that there is a general agreement among people as to what they consider to be the right way of acting. This becomes the right way of acting. This of course is a complete denial of any dogmatic basis for morality.

Humanism, as its name suggests, makes a great deal of human values. These are their own validation. They do not need validation from other objective standards, and here we immediately come up against one of the radical differences between Humanism and Christianity. It has sometimes been suggested that Humanists are opposed to the Church but not opposed to Christ. This attractive idea is really exploded if we notice what, in fact, the Humanists are saying. Blackham discusses this question of the basis of moral decisions, urges that there is no need for any objective standard, and on this ground rejects the claims of Christ. 'Christ is the archetype of unqualified submission and obedience to the Will of God . . . It is impossible to follow Christ on any other terms, and the Humanist finds the acceptance of these terms a violation of himself and his whole experience. His rejection of Christ is therefore categorical.'[1] In view of that quotation, it seems difficult to understand what is meant by the statement on the dust cover of the volume quoted that it may mark the end of the cold war between

[1] *Op. Cit.*, p. 18.

Christians and Humanists. A more realistic view is expressed by Margaret Knight interviewed in connection with the Humanist Week of 1967: 'The humanist *raison d'être* is to put across the view that the good life can be lived without the aid of any supernatural belief. The main thing liberal organizations are up against is the organized opposition of the Church.'[1] We therefore see that the humanist position is a clear denial of the claims of Christian orthodoxy with regard to the basis of moral decisions, for no Christian can categorically reject Christ.

Furthermore, modern Humanism is a clear denial of any belief in a supernatural power beyond Man. Blackham writes in *Religion in a Modern Society*, 'Humanism is a practical decision to live on the assumption that man is on his own and this life is all'.[2] The slogan for the Humanist Week of 1967 was 'This life is all we have; make it a good one'. As Margaret Knight puts it in her contribution to *The Humanist Anthology*, 'Humanism sees no reason for believing in a supernatural God'. All this, I think, makes it abundantly clear that although Humanists are inclined not to talk much about their metaphysical belief, when this is uncovered it is quite apparent that it is atheistic. In the humanist view there is nothing beyond empirical experience. Until recently Humanists have taken this position so much for granted that they have not bothered to state the grounds on which their scepticism rests. Recently Antony Flew has written an up-to-date critique of Christian orthodox belief in *God and Philosophy*. Flew's argument is that philosophy must act as a sort of magistrate, not advocating any particular view, but adjudicating between rival claims. He takes the orthodox statements of Christian belief as representative and asserts that the view of God which such statements as the Thirty Nine Articles contain is manifestly untenable. This is in part due to inherent inconsistencies between the theistic definitions and common experience. Thus, if God is the Creator in the proper meaning of the word, all things must be in his control, and therefore man cannot have any choice. But it is a clear fact of experience that man does have choice. So experience contradicts the theistic assertion. Again, if God is wholly good, and also all-powerful, there should not be any evil in the world, for evil is by definition

[1] *The Observer*, 29 October 1967.
[2] p. 113.

contrary to the good will of God. But there manifestly is evil in the world. So the idea of a good and omnipotent God must be abandoned in the light of experience. Further, the usual view of theists is that both natural and revealed knowledge of God can be accepted. It is true that some theologians (Karl Barth, for instance) deny the validity of natural knowledge, but this is not the commonly-held view, especially among Roman Catholic theologians, whom Flew is particularly anxious to refute. But, alleges Flew, natural and revealed knowledge are not complementary; they are contradictory. Revealed knowledge denies the supremacy of reason, on which natural knowledge is based. We can't have both; and a reasonable man must continue to accept the authority of reason, and cannot therefore at the same time rely on revelation. Natural theology has always been recognized to fall short of certainty about God, and reason demands that agnosticism is the only live option.

Flew also shows that many of the arguments commonly employed to support theism are invalid. The allegation that everything manifests purpose, and the only sufficient purpose for the universe is God, fails to convince those who see purpose as only applicable to human affairs, and who argue that the idea of purpose is imposed on events by human thought, but is not really inherent in the events themselves. The common assertion that without the idea of God the world is meaningless can be answered by asking whether it is necessary to posit only one meaning to this highly complicated universe. And there is no truth, Professor Flew says, in the facile assertion that morality collapses if theism is denied. And as for the assertion that belief in God is a source of comfort for many people, this means that we can believe in anything which gives comfort to us, whether it is true or false. Another fairly common support for belief in God arises out of a consideration of religious experience, which is said to be 'self-authenticating'. To this Flew replies that if religious experience is *self*-authenticating it cannot point to the authenticity of God; if on the other hand it is claimed that God, an external reality, authenticates the experience, plainly it is not self-authenticating. Flew concludes the whole argument by reiterating the Stratonician presumption, that the universe is everything that there is. Theologians, he says, are too ready to assume that the edifices of doctrine

which they construct are about something which really exists;
they rarely stop to ask if there is any substance at all behind
their complicated assertions.

Such a thoroughgoing critique of theism requires a much
fuller answer than can be attempted in this context. It serves a
very useful purpose, however, even before it is answered or
refuted, by showing that some of the well-known arguments
for theism just do not stand up. Too often Christian apologetic
rests on assumptions which cannot be maintained, like the
universality of purpose, or the necessity of a first cause. But it
would be wrong to imply that this is not realized by any
Christian thinkers. There has been a great deal of clarification
of thinking about God among theologians in recent years, and
a serious discussion of this subject must take into account
modern developments as well as traditional formulations. To
these contemporary theologians Flew's arguments must seem
rather naive, not only because he seems to give no credence to
anything except cold reason, but also because he seems unaware of the developments in the understanding of God, which
do indeed owe a great deal to contemporary philosophy. Flew
appears to assume that 'God' ought to be demonstrable either
by reason or by empirical tests. But this has never been accepted
by Christian thinkers. Significantly, most of the classic arguments about the being of God have been advanced by men who
did not begin with a vacuum which they hoped to fill with God.
Rather, like Anselm, they first believed in God, and then
sought reasons for what they already believed. Christians must
not use this approach to nullify all debate about God; we must
keep in touch with sceptics, for their questions are real, and in
answering them we may often reach clearer light on our own
faith. Yet in the end we believe in God, not because we think
we can prove his existence, nor because we have empirical
demonstration, but because the totality of our experience
points to that which is beyond reason and sense experience,
perhaps partly describable as that which gives coherence and
integration to our whole life.

Along with this scepticism about the supernatural, a characteristic of many Humanists is their serious attitude to human
problems and possibilities. Being by nature anti-dogmatic,
Humanism is not committed to any one ethical principle, any

more than it looks to any single person as its exemplar. The overriding concern is that each man should express in his own situation that natural excellence which is his own endowment. This should be concerned for the public good, not merely the happiness of the individual. But the happiness principle is not to be decried; it is indeed man's right and responsibility to be happy, and here humanist ideas are most opposed to those traditional religious attitudes which regarded happiness as a sin, and inculcated a very gloomy and restrictive attitude to life. Certainly many Humanists show a strong and passionate concern for human welfare; and this is having a noticeable effect on Christian ideas. A good example of this insistence on the importance of human affairs is the way in which the old saying 'outside the Church there is no salvation' is now interpreted by many Christians as 'apart from the world there is no salvation'.

One of the chief virtues of the Humanist, according to Blackham, is tolerance. He approves of Voltaire's idea that tolerance expresses a permanent truth of the human condition. It is true, as Blackham points out, that tolerance can be ineffective in recognizing and opposing evil; this was the charge levelled against many Frenchmen during the Nazi occupation by Jean-Paul Sartre. Clearly tolerance must be accompanied by vigilance, and frequently the question must arise whether to tolerate evil is not to encourage it. But generally speaking Christians would agree that tolerance is a splendid virtue; certainly intolerance should be recognized as one of the chief enemies of good human relations, and it is human relations that most ethical issues are really about.

Blackham is sensitive to the criticism that Humanism is mainly an intellectual attitude, and as we shall see in a moment, he goes to considerable trouble to refute the view that these ideas have no relevance to ordinary people. It is a good thing for Christians to recognize that the same charge is being made against them—especially against new theologians. It is said, by Christians and non-Christians, that most of the problems being faced by new theology are really pseudo problems, only significant to a very small proportion of believers, and entirely irrelevant to non-believers. No doubt there is a big gap between modern thinking and ordinary believing, but I suggest that both Christians and Humanists do need their thinkers. Without intellectual advance any attitude to life eventually atrophies; this is as true for Humanism as it is for Christianity.

To answer the charge of intellectualism, Blackham asserts that many people do in fact take up a humanist position without knowing it. The attraction of Humanism for them is that it makes articulate what they themselves have come to believe, and they find that the Humanists are really speaking for them when they talk of the impossibility of believing in the super-natural, the irrelevance of any idea of life after death, and the inability of religions to give any proper guidance in moral questions. 'The simplest people will for themselves think that we don't know and can't know about ultimate things, that ethics are much the most important and certain part of the great religions and say much the same in all of them, that if you don't know the difference between right and wrong the parson can't tell you, that we should respect other people's convictions and way of life; that the Bible should be judged by common sense and moral sense; that it is reasonable to co-operate in a society which is regulated to serve the interests of all and not merely of the few or of some, that this is the only life we are sure of and we better make the most of it.'[1]

Or to take another example: quite often in modern novels a humanist attitude is expressed without being given that name. For instance, in *A Kind of Loving*, by Stan Barstow, there is a rather commonplace story of a boy-girl relationship. The girl eventually discovers that she is going to have a baby and so they get married, only to lose the unborn child in a miscarriage when the girl falls downstairs. This naturally leaves the young man with a certain sense of frustration and defeat. Towards the end of the book he soliloquizes as follows: 'Now I reckon I've got a lot of things weighed up. All this has taught me about life and everything, I mean, and the way I see it is this; the secret of it all is that there is no secret, and no God, and no heaven and no hell, and if you say, well, what is life all about, I'll say its about life, and that's all, and its enough.'[2]

It should be clear from these quotations that in attempting to engage in a dialogue with Humanists, the Christian apologist

---

[1] *Objections to Humanism*, p. 23.
[2] *A Kind of Loving*, p. 272.

is not merely considering a very small intellectual sector of society. There is little doubt, I think, that the humanist attitude, articulate or inarticulate, is very popular among large sections of the community. This is the context in which Christian assertions must be made. This is also the context in which religious education must be given in schools. The background of many of our children is this Humanism; often hardly thought out at all. The assumptions about morals, about the irrelevance of religion and the necessity of making the best you can of this life because there isn't any other—these assumptions are continually being made by the parents of many of our children.

It is interesting further to note that among Humanists there are considerable differences of opinion as to what should now be their line of advance. Some argue for the construction of a humanist metaphysical system; others think that this would be a great tragedy for Humanism, which is essentially a free and undogmatic attitude. Indeed, many people whose point of view is certainly approximately humanist, will not even call themselves Humanists because they think that their attitude ought not to be systematized or documented in any way. These people think that a metaphysic would be the end of Humanism. Humanism, some further claim, may operate within religion, cleansing and perhaps rectifying its errors. But Humanism is not properly a religion. It is unworldly worldliness, or impassioned materialism. Blackham sums up organized Humanism as follows: 'Organized Humanism is a general association with no specific object, a fellowship in shared general assumptions and shared general aims.'[1] The one point on which Blackham is very insistent is that Humanism is an attitude which involves a commitment to these aims and objectives: 'Unbelief, without any effort to help to shoulder the consequences for mankind is not Humanism.'[2]

As I have already indicated, it is not easy to discover from humanist statements what are the main bases of their beliefs, but by taking account of contemporary humanist writing, which is quite voluminous, it is possible to clarify the humanist attitude as follows:

[1] *Objections to Humanism*, p. 26.
[2] *Ibid.*, p. 27.

1. There is no supernatural.
2. There is no life beyond this present one.
3. Morals don't need religion.
4. Life is to be lived to its fullest extent.

It will be noted that the first three of these assertions are, in fact, negative. This is in spite of the claim of Humanism to be a positive approach to life—which claim incidentally is one of its chief attractions to young people. In effect, on these three points Humanism is really old agnosticism or atheism put in a modern form. It is, after all, to a very large extent a negative attitude and in that sense a restricting attitude.

The question which remains for us to discuss is what is to be the Christian attitude to these humanist assertions? There are some, of course, who regard Humanism as the chief opponent of Christianity and believe that there should be a new crusade against it with a view to eliminating it altogether. At the other extreme there are those who think that the points on which there are differences between Humanism and Christianity are of small importance compared with matters on which there is agreement. So that the attitude of the Christian should be co-operation with the Humanist in all his good intentions, and not too much concern about different attitudes to questions about the nature of things which after all may not be easy to clarify and which don't seem to make much difference to the everyday business of living.

My suggestion lies somewhere between these two extremes. I want to suggest that we need to be clear about the differences between Humanism and Christianity whether we claim to follow one or other of these attitudes. There can be no advantage to either point of view in a confusion which blurs any differences which really do exist. Along with this clarity I think we do need a high degree of sensitive awareness of each other's convictions.

Taking, then, these humanist attitudes in turn, we notice first that Humanism is an assertion that there is no supernatural—a practical decision on the assumption that man is on his own and this life is all. To a Humanist this blanket denial of the supernatural includes a denial of the existence of God. This attitude is often supported by a scientific scepticism which asserts that only those realities which are empirically knowable are in any sense real, and furthermore that modern philosophy has made it impossible to give any credence to the assertion of the existence of God. Can a Christian accept this point of view? We must leave until later in this discussion the question of what the Christian can now say about God. There is no doubt that this is a very live issue at the moment and we cannot merely repeat the things which have been said in the past, but I venture to suggest even at this stage in the argument that the Christian must be able to say something about God. Without an assertion of the reality of God, Christianity ceases to be what it has always claimed to be. It may use the same name for a different attitude, but we cannot fail to recognize that without belief in God Christianity is not what Christianity has always claimed to be. We ought to notice that the Christian belief in God does not involve belief in a general group of supposed realities called 'the supernatural'. The question does not necessarily concern the existence of the supernatural; the Christian is only called upon to assert the existence of God, and how a Christian can assert this and what he means by this assertion we must leave to a later chapter. But we do, I think, have to be quite clear that whatever the new theologians may say about the death of God and the problem of not being able to use old theological language, for most people the Christian faith still involves belief in God. Here, then, there is immediately a radical difference between Christians and Humanists, a difference which cannot by any means be glossed over by any amount of tolerance or understanding from either side.

The second negation of Humanism is with regard to life after death. This life is all and it is enough, say the Humanists. 'Leave the hereafter to the eager believers. Join the Humanists to cope with the here and now', as one of their clever slogans has put it. The reason for the humanist denial of the life after death is supposedly scientific. They argue that our experience of life is always of life in a body, that is, in the physical environment. Everyone knows that at death the physical body ceases to exist. Humanists therefore argue that it is impossible for any life to continue after death. The conditions of life are physical existence and at the end of physical existence life must come to an end. They are not impressed by the argument that it is sometimes claimed there is a general desire for life beyond the grave. Quite apart from the possibility that this is not a general desire, they argue that this does not prove the reality of a life beyond the grave. This desire for life after death is really the desire for more life; we desire more of that which we have already experienced. Humanists also argue that it is quite intolerable to suppose that our morality must somehow depend upon a system of reward and punishment in a supposed future existence. The Humanist bravely faces the fact that, when he dies, that is the end of him. He may believe that values and even aspirations continue in the human race, but as far as he is concerned death is the end. 'When I die I shall rot and nothing of my ego will survive' (Bertrand Russell). In denying the possibility of a life after death the Humanist reckons he has really cut the lifeline of religion. He believes that it is this desire for life after death, or a desire to come to terms with the fear of death, that is the real basis of religion. So if the question of what happens after I am dead can be answered with a simple 'nothing', then the whole reason for religion collapses.

In this situation the Christian is in considerable difficulty. It used to be clear that belief in life after death was one of the cardinal beliefs of the Christian faith. Indeed, if we go back into the last century, it is fairly evident that belief in life after death was so generally accepted that evangelists used this idea as a very strong lever to persuade their hearers to accept their message. There was a vivid sense of a future destiny including, of course, the possibility of hell and damnation for those who were not saved. This situation is now radically changed. There are, apparently, some people within the Church, as well as many outside, who really do not believe that there is any significant meaning in life after death. It is noticeable that modern theologians have written very little on this subject. A few years ago I heard an American theologian say that of the theological teachers he knew not more than perhaps five per cent were prepared to say that they believed in life after death. Should the Christian then agree with the humanist assertion and abandon his belief in life beyond the grave?

There are some Christians who would take this point of view. Others see that without coming to terms with the problems of death as well as life, human existence is often completely meaningless. It isn't a question of whether or not we think this present life is important. It is more a question of 'Can we make sense of this life unless we can see it in an eternal setting?' And there are certainly many moral problems like injustice, cruelty and lack of opportunity which deny the morality of the universe unless we can believe that after this life there is another life in which God can bless those who have had so little blessing in this present existence. For in this life evil does go unpunished and goodness unrecognized. One of the features of modern theology with regard to this doctrine is an emphasis upon the resurrection rather than immortality. Christian orthodoxy until quite recently was limited to the idea that at creation man was made an immortal soul. This immortal soul quite literally could not be destroyed. Therefore its destiny must be either eternal blessedness or eternal misery. This idea really springs from a Greek notion of the soul and its indestructible nature. It presents great problems, especially from a philosophical point of view, because it seems to regard the soul as a substance. Biblical scholars have increasingly argued that the attitude of the New Testament is not that man's soul is immortal, but rather that through the activity of God in Christ, man is given the possibility of eternal life with God. The emphasis, therefore, falls upon the act of God in Christ in raising Christ from the dead. This is the first fruit of man's hope of life after death, and the continuation of man's hope is in the fact that through Christ risen from the dead man is in a new relationship to God and may then, in that relationship, hope to live on beyond this life. Those Christians who believe in a future life do so, I think, mainly because they find it impossible to believe that the relationship with God in Christ that they have known in this life can be ended by the mere incident of physical death.

The further emphasis of modern theology in connection with the doctrine of the future life is that the teaching of the New Testament is certainly very much in favour of the connection between this life and the future life. There is no basis whatever in the New Testament for the idea that we can neglect our responsibilities in this life in order to obtain a greater blessedness hereafter; rather the New Testament makes it abundantly clear that if we do not find life with God in Christ here we have precious little hope of finding it hereafter. It seems as if this is

another point on which Christianity and Humanism must agree
to differ, for it is traditionally a very important part of the
Christian faith to be able to say 'I believe in the resurrection of
the body and life everlasting.'

How this is related to the teaching in schools is a relevant
matter because, rather surprisingly, young people are often
more interested in this question of future destiny than older
people. The psychological reason for this may be that when we
are young we feel able to think about this subject dispassion-
ately because it is remote from us. When we get older we know
only too well that it is becoming a real issue and we hang on to
this present life, seeing that there is not much of it left. It may
be that this aspect of the Christian faith is particularly relevant
to young people, and if this belief is any guide and inspiration
for our present and future activities in this life, then teaching
about the future life should certainly be included in our
presentation of the Christian faith.

On the question of morality, there is apparently a great deal
of common ground between Humanists and Christians. The
Humanist is insistent on the importance of human relations and
he believes that only actions which are based on love can be
right; there is no need of any external sanction or any absolute
standard. Morality is adaptable to changing human needs, and
providing we act in love we are bound to be acting in accor-
dance with the highest standard of which we are capable. The
Humanist morality is often positive and revolutionary; it seems
to be concerned with matters of great moment to mankind, and
in this often seems to be preferable to the Christian morality
which looks rather negative and frequently seems to be concerned only with peripheral matters. Concern about abortion
law reform and the just treatment of homosexuals; the need for
divorce law reform and so on, are at the moment very much to
the fore in humanist thinking. But Christianity also bases its
morality upon love. It would be fairly easy to say that Christian
love is of a different quality from that considered by the
Humanists, but this would only lead to confusion. The Christian view of morality is based upon love; love as we know it
among human beings, but recognizing that this is only an
inadequate and undeveloped form of love. The Christian is
not opposed to the humanist emphasis upon love. He is bound

5

to point out that it is by no means easy to determine what is a loving attitude. To a Christian, love is personified in Christ. This means that we have a standard whereby we can judge the validity of human love. A realistic attitude to human nature will always remind us that it is possible for people to be very self-deceived about their attitude. There is a great deal of self-love which cannot be avoided; but in Christ we see one who truly did live for others, who carried out through faithfulness and loyalty—even to the extent of dying on the Cross—an attitude of complete love for all mankind. This is the Christian standard. It does not mean that there are simple rules to be applied in every situation. The Christian still has to work out, often in conjunction with his fellow Christians, what are the demands of a loving attitude, but he does find these demands exemplified and fortified in the living presence of Christ whom he knows through his faith. The Christian is not, I think, at all committed to the idea of an unchanging, dogmatic morality. Indeed, there are plenty of suggestions in the New Testament and in Christian history that the Christian view of morality must develop and can indeed be regarded as changing according to changing circumstances of human life. The difference then between Humanists and Christians on the question of morality is mainly on the basis of what really constitutes a loving attitude and how man can hope to reach anywhere near the standards which love sets for him.

The fourth aspect of humanist conviction which must be considered in comparison with Christianity is the humanist optimism about human prospects. The Humanist sees before man a very bright prospect indeed. He recognizes that at the moment there are certain great difficulties and dangers facing the human race, concerned with war and poverty, racial discrimination and similar great issues. He also recognizes that man is still much inhibited by the lingering religious ideas which he has inherited from his past. But assuming that the threat of war can be removed, and poverty can be overcome, and assuming that religion slips quietly away into oblivion, the Humanist believes that mankind is marching forward to an upland of great achievement and fulfilment. This present period of human activity is regarded as the welfare state. The Humanist looks forward to the fulfilment state when man will be able to develop fully his potentialities of interest in art and music and nature and all the many activities which are open to him. On this particular issue it looks as if the development of automation will make possible a much shorter working life for most people, and this could be the means whereby man can reach a fulfilment state.

The Christian attitude to this is not to scorn it, nor to think that it is an impossible utopian dream. It is true that the Christian is bound to see the dark side as well as the bright side of human life. The Christian should remind himself that a great deal of this idea of the fulfilment state only makes sense in the western world and indeed only in part of the western world. A very large proportion of the world is still not by any means up to the welfare state, let alone the fulfilment state; and we must be very careful not to suppose that everyone in the world is living as comfortable and fulfilled a life as we are able to do in our civilized western society. Again, the Christian is bound to take note of the frailty and selfishness of mankind which can so easily spoil the bright prospects the Humanist talks about. Maybe it is true that Christianity has been too pessimistic about man's potentiality and his prospects. I shall be referring to this more fully in the next chapter. But it would be foolhardy not to recognize that, human nature being what it is, it is by no means as easy as falling off a log for mankind to advance to the pleasant uplands that the Humanist talks about.

There is, nevertheless, much that the Christian can learn from the humanist optimism. It is undoubtedly true that this optimism has not been very evident in the Churches of late. Our message about man seems often to be rather depressing and negative. We have not realized the possibility of man's advance. Christianity has been presented too often as backward-looking rather than forward-looking. We have forgotten the words of Christ, that he came that men might have life and have it more fully. Christianity has much to learn from Humanism about human prospects. If it is right for the Christian to charge the Humanist with being foolishly optimistic about human nature, it is equally right for the Humanist to charge the Christian with being foolishly pessimistic. Certainly as far as human prospects are concerned there are often very real possibilities of co-operation between Humanists and Christians in order that these hopes may be fulfilled, and man's future may be brighter than his past has been.

Having briefly set out the differences between Humanism and Christianity, we are faced with the issue of how to decide between these two alternatives. The purpose of this book is not to present a detailed argument as to the advantages of Christianity against Humanism.[1] All that need be said here is that there are some clear convictions to be dealt with on both sides. It is certainly no part of a Christian attitude to impugn the sincerity of people who take up the humanist position. As far as we can we should be willing to work with all men of goodwill. There must be continuing debate between Humanists and Christians and there must certainly be continuing co-operation on all good projects.

Nevertheless, the responsibility of the Christian is surely to present the truth as he sees it and as he has received it through his Christian tradition. This is the basis for the conviction that religious education in schools should continue to have a Christian foundation. Those who argue that religious education is mere religious indoctrination and should cease are arguing for the abandonment of a part of our heritage which has been extremely valuable in the past. It certainly seems true, whatever the vociferous humanist minority may say, that most parents still wish their children to be taught the Christian way of life. I would therefore think that the response of Christians to the humanist challenge about R.E. is not to agree that R.E. should be abandoned in favour of what I suppose you would call M.E. (that is, Moral Education). This, of course, would have equally serious difficulties regarding curriculum and differences of opinion and charges of indoctrination. The attitude of a Christian, I think, should be that we ought to improve our methods of religious education, not abandon them. This, of course, will not meet the criticisms of the Humanist, for he does not seem to be criticising us for being ineffective but for being too effective. Nevertheless, the challenge before Christian teachers is to make the teaching of the Christian faith far more meaningful to children than it is at present, and in order to do this I think it is useful to think through again the basic asser-

---

[1] I may perhaps be permitted to refer to my *The Christian Approach to the Humanist*, which is a fuller exposition of my views.

tions of the Christian faith, and this is what we shall try to do in the remainder of this book. For it is my conviction that only a radical re-appraisal of the Christian faith will be adequate to meet the challenges of our situation. Old orthodox Christianity cannot any longer hope to present the faith in a way which twentieth-century man can understand or live by. Not for the first time in its history the Church is being forced to reconsider its teaching in the light of contemporary developments.

4 | *Starting Again with Man*

THE combined efforts of new theology and Humanism have effectively demolished most of old orthodox Christianity. But after demolition comes rebuilding. Where shall we begin to rebuild? Theology traditionally starts with God, and in the past we have been warned of the danger of any other beginning. For instance, in an essay written in 1924, Bultmann wrote: 'The subject of theology is *God* and the chief charge to be brought against liberal theology is that it has dealt not with God but with man. God means the radical negation and sublimation of man.'[1] This warning was very necessary because of the way that liberal theology became too man-centred. Its motto almost became 'Glory to man in the highest, for man is the master of things'. And yet in spite of these warnings, I think we have to look again at this question of beginning with man. There are two reasons, in my view, for starting at this point.

Firstly, in the same essay quoted above, Bultmann also writes as follows: 'Theology speaks of God because it speaks of man as he stands before God. That is, theology speaks out of faith.'[2] This assertion, contradictory though it may seem to Bultmann's former statement, is, I would submit, profoundly true. We do not discover truth about God by trying to think of God in isolation from man. In a remarkable paper Karl Barth refers to

[1] R. Bultmann, *Faith and Understanding*, S.C.M. Press, p. 29.
[2] *Ibid.*, p. 52.

The Humanity of God. This means that God has committed himself to man for ever; if a man is to know anything about God,
he will find it among men. God is to be found among men,
not in separation from men. It seems to me that there is a sound
theological basis for saying that we must begin with man and,
from our consideration of man, we may indeed be able to
arrive at some sound conclusions regarding the nature of God.

The second reason for this approach through man is that we
have available to us a large amount of understanding of human
nature through such human sciences as anthropology, psychology, and sociology. These sciences are based on observation.
They use the scientific method, and they bring us increasing
knowledge in the field of human nature and human behaviour.
There seems to be, therefore, a real possibility that we shall
gain knowledge in this field. If, on the other hand, we begin
with God, not only do most of us find knowledge here very
difficult to discover, but it is also true that the dogmatic assertions about God, and man in relation to God, may very well
conceal insight into the reality of human nature. The traditional
dogmatic theological approach which begins with God and then
sees man in the context of God can very easily cause us to think
that the choice before us is either to be scientific or dogmatic.
This gives rise to an increasing gap between scientific knowledge and theological knowledge, a gap which is little short of a
tragedy in our time. Instead of it being possible for the believer
in God to see his place in the modern world, and to see how he
can use all free knowledge which is available to him, it seems
very often as if the believer is faced with the choice of being
either a believer or a twentieth-century man, but not both.
This is a most unfortunate conclusion and is bound to lead to
a continued lessening of the influence of religious faith.

This dichotomy between science and faith has many unfortunate results. It means for one thing that faith seems always to
be fighting a rearguard action which it continually loses, and
the whole religious attitude has seemed to become more and
more irrelevant and more and more obscure. We only have to
ask ourselves what real relevance there is in the dogmatic point
of view that man is corrupt and unable to save himself. Many of
us accept these ideas as assumptions which are unquestioned,
but I would suggest that they do not, in fact, make much

difference to the way we live our life or to our understanding of human nature. But perhaps the greater tragedy of this dichotomy between science and faith is that the help faith might be able to render to modern scientific man it is precluded from rendering because of the gap which has widened between the two approaches. If the view of faith has any truth in it, it will certainly be an impoverishment for the scientific attitude to be without it. There may be situations in the not too distant future where this could become really serious. Take, for instance, the attitude of Dr Leach in his 1967 Reith Lectures: Leach argues that man is now able to be a god and he has to learn to act in a properly divine way. Now we may want to question some of the assumptions lying behind this idea; but in so far as Leach means that the responsibility for human future development rests fairly and squarely upon human shoulders, I do not think that he is saying anything that is contrary to Christian faith. Man will have to decide not only how to cope with his environment, but how to change it. But then the question arises, on what basis can man agree as to the right changes to be made in, say, the structure of the natural world, or the determination of the sex of our children? Who decides these matters? It seems to me that this idea of man being in control of his destiny requires a sense of unity and a sense of value—both points on which the Christian view ought to be making a great contribution to modern understanding. But so long as we remain separated from those who are presenting a scientific point of view, we are precluded from making this contribution.

So I recognize the risk involved in starting with man, but I insist that that is where our theological reconstruction must begin. We begin our theological restatement not in the realm of a strict theological discussion, but in the realm of science, particularly the realm of the human sciences. We must, I submit, use the insights of modern science in order to understand what is the truth about human nature. I am not arguing that we must necessarily accept everything that these sciences say about man. When they are making assertions about facts which can be scientifically investigated and scientifically verified or falsified, I do think we have to accept these scientific statements. It is when we come to questions of interpretation and value judgement that we have to use scientific knowledge in the light of our own understanding of the theological judgements which we gain through the life of faith.

This approach through a consideration of what science is saying about man is all the more hopeful in our present situation because recently several very competent scientists have written on the subject of the nature of man, and in giving us the benefit of their scientific knowledge have related this knowledge to Christian principles. I am thinking of authors like Sir Alister Hardy (*The Living Stream* and *The Divine Flame*); W. H. Thorpe, (*Science, Man and Morals* and *Biology and the Nature of Man*); David Lack, (*Evolutionary Theory and Christian Belief*); Teilhard de Chardin, (*The Phenomenon of Man*); and also the book edited by Ian Ramsey (*Biology & Personality*).

What I am suggesting at this point is that instead of looking at man through Augustinian spectacles and seeing him as a depraved, fallen, and largely hopeless creature, we leave aside these presuppositions and look at man firstly as modern sciences are revealing him, and then go on to see how these views relate to modern theological understanding.

The question then is, what are the basic ideas which these human sciences are asserting about human nature? One often gets the impression from popular expositions that scientists are pessimistic about man's nature and his future. In one sense, of course, it is true that a great deal of pessimism is justified when one considers the possibility of atomic and nuclear warfare, or when, for instance, one considers the threat of over-population, or the dangers of germ warfare, and other equally-terrible prognostications about the future. The general impression often given is that the scientist is an inhuman creature who is quite indifferent to the true human life of which he is no longer a part. Now a study of a modern biology is a very good antidote to this sort of pessimism. The attitude of many biologists is basically optimistic about man's situation and his prospects. Consider on the one hand the question of the relative insignificance of man in this vast universe which science has made known to us. This can be, of course, quite understandably the basis for a pessimistic attitude; but the human scientists remind us that it is wrong to be too impressed by size; and human sciences have revealed that there is about man a quality which is not found elsewhere in the natural world. They do, indeed, insist again and again on the uniqueness of man. The days are gone when the main object of biology was to show that man was only an animal and was not basically different from all other animals. The basis on which the difference between man and even the higher animals is delineated is, for instance, that in man alone is there a unitary mind and the capacity to correlate abstract principles. In this way human science is supporting Christian convictions about the uniqueness and significance of man.

Or again, take the fear that many people have that we are now capable of making machines which will eventually be able to do all that we can do, and the more complex and sophisticated they become the more we are in danger of being slaves to them. It is often said, for instance, that before long computers will be made which will be able to perform all the tasks of which man is capable and all the processes of human thought will be in that sense computerized. Karl Popper makes it quite clear that this comparison between a computer and a person is false. Brains don't think. Only persons think, and however highly sophisticated a computer may become, it will never be a person. There is a good deal of false analogy being made between computers and people. Again, a proper understanding of what is involved in human nature reassures us about the uniqueness and the wonder of human nature.

The complexity of human nature is very marvellously revealed in various ways. One of the most eminent of modern geneticists, Thoday, has written as follows: 'Biological progress not only involves increasing versatility of individual species but also increasing diversity of species harmoniously adapted to one another.'[1] This complexity is seen in various ways in connection with the fairly recent discovery of D.N.A. This is the substance through which our genetical inheritance is passed on from one generation to another. The marvel of this process, and the way in which so rarely are mistakes made in the transmitting of information through the generations can be noticed in the following statement by the scientist Dobzhansky: 'All the biological evolution extending over a period of some two billion years has occurred on the level of genetic "words" and

[1] Quoted by W. H. Thorpe, *Science, Man and Morals*, p. 117.

"sentences"; no new "letters" have been added or, as far as is known, lost.'[1] The genetic alphabet, Dobzhansky says, is composed of not more than four letters. It is almost unbelievable that so complicated a code of genetical information can be passed on with such accuracy through so simple a mechanism. All this reminds us of what Thorpe calls 'the staggeringly complex system of nervous cells in the brain'.[2]

Or again, notice the way in which biological sciences are investigating the meaning of life. The question 'what is life?' is not only the title of a now rather dated popular song; it is also a very significant question for scientists to ask. Recent experiments in deep freezing, called anabiosis, show that it is possible to suspend all activity over quite a long period by means of low temperature. When the right conditions are restored, there is a reactivation which shows that the essence of life is still present. The conclusion that the scientists draw from this is that the essence of life is not activity but structure, and if life is essentially structural, Thorpe says, it is reasonable to expect that artificial production of life by man will take place, 'within the not very distant future'. This possibility of the artificial creation of life ought not to fill us with holy horror; it ought to help us to recognize that there is within man a very great deal of potential skill in dealing with his life.

The next question to raise, then, is how do these scientific assertions which have been briefly outlined team up with theological affirmations? We ought firstly be quite clear as to the status of the theological affirmations relative to the scientific ones. The theological affirmations are not about extra facts which are not discoverable by science. Theological affirmations are matters of interpretation and integration. We must not think that there is available to the theologian a secret area of fact which is not accessible to the scientist. This is not the way that theology can help in the modern understanding of man. Rather, it is in the question of interpretation, integration, and application that the theological assertions become relevant in our modern situations. You will notice that I am assuming that there is no question of basic antagonism between the scientific and theological assertions. What I am suggesting is that the

[1] Quoted by W. H. Thorpe, *Science, Man and Morals*, Methuen, p. 12.
[2] W. H. Thorpe, *Biology and Nature of Man*, Oxford University Press, p. 26.

scientific assertions are the basis on which the theological statements about man must be made.

We then turn to the Bible to see what elements of interpretation and integration can be discovered from the biblical statements about man. It is not possible in this discussion to set out in
any detail a summary of the biblical teaching about man, but
I want to highlight some of the emphases which seem to me to
have been forgotten in recent theology. The Bible several times
makes the assertion that man is made in the image of God. We
tend to forget the significance of this because it is overlaid with
the idea of man being a fallen creature. Let me remind you
firstly of what is said in Psalm 8. The Psalm begins with a statement about the majesty of God and in wonder at the way in
which God is at all concerned with so small a creature as man.
'What is man that thou art mindful of him?'—and then it goes
on—'Yet thou hast made him little less than God, and dost
crown him with glory and honour. Thou hast given him
dominion over the works of thy hands; thou hast put all things
under his feet'—and notice that the Psalm finishes—'O Lord,
our Lord, how majestic is thy name in all the earth!' This
seems to me to suggest that the consideration of the nature of
man will very often lead to a sincere ascription of praise to God
the Creator of man. This idea of the importance of man and
his need to remember his own significance is also very well
expressed in the Book of Job. Towards the end of that long
discussion between Job and his friends about the problem of
suffering and Job's refusal to accept the traditional explana-
tions, the Lord answered Job—'Who is this that darkens
counsel by words without knowledge? Gird up your loins like a
man. I will question you and you shall declare to me' (Job
38: 2, 3 and 40: 6, 7.) The same idea of the significance of man
and his dignity is expressed in Psalm 115 v. 16. 'The heavens
are the Lord's heavens, but the earth he has given to the sons
of men.' All these Old Testament references, it seems to me,
insist that man is in a unique position. He must remember his
dignity and his mopirtance because that is how God has made
him.

When we consider the gospels, we must surely remember not
only such a saying as 'the Sabbath was made for man and not
man for the Sabbath' but indeed the whole reality of the

Incarnation. The whole meaning of the assertion 'the Word became flesh' is a declaration of the significance of human nature. It was, let us remember, human flesh that the Word became, not any other sort of flesh. Again, think of the views expressed in the first chapter of the letter to the Colossians. Christ is the agent in creation; through him a new creation and a new human race will be inaugurated. This, again, speaks of the high dignity of man. And furthermore, this emphasis upon man's dignity and importance, and the result of the Incarnation in giving man freedom and responsibility is expressed in the discussion about faith and sonship of God in Galations 3 and 4. 'Now that faith has come, the tutor's charge is at an end. For through faith you are all sons of God in union with Christ Jesus . . . When the term was completed, God sent his own Son, born of a woman, born under the law . . . in order that we might attain the status of sons. To prove that you are sons, God has sent into our hearts the Spirit of his Son crying, "Abba, Father!"; you are therefore no longer a slave but a son, and if a son, then also by God's own act an heir.' (NEB). This is the basic meaning of the idea that man has come of age. This notion of man's majority is often expressed nowadays in terms of twentieth-century development of knowledge; man has become so knowledgeable and so clever that in this sense he has come of age. But Paul puts it not in the twentieth-century but in the first. It is because Christ has come that man has come of age. In Christ God has given man freedom to become his sons by faith, so that we are no longer to think of ourselves as servants and people without responsibility; we are to realize that God has said, in effect, 'You are now capable of taking responsibility on the earth which is yours to use and to inhabit; you are capable of acting according to your free sonship.' Tragically, the situation has very often been that we have said to God that we are afraid of this responsibility; we are sure that we shall make a mess of the world if it's left to us; but God has resolutely affirmed that success is possible for us and he has given us the opportunity—and indeed the need—to go on and possess the earth in freedom as his sons.

This idea of man's nature and his uniqueness and freedom is being strongly emphasized by modern theology. For instance, the theologians who have an existential emphasis are now

insisting that it is the quality of man's existence which distin-
guishes him from all other creatures. It is because man exists
that he is so significant. Macquarrie and Tillich both speak
about the existential truth of man's nature before God. Now it
wouldn't be true to say that these existential theologians ignore
the potential evil or the inadequacy of human nature. Tillich,
for instance, using the ideas of Heidegger, asserts that man has
the responsibility of moving from inauthentic to authentic
existence. That is, from a life dominated by fear and frustration,
to a fully human life of freedom and responsibility. This movement is a movement which can only take place through the
attitude of faith and trust in God, but it is nevertheless a movement which is possible and which is indeed taking place. So the
existentialist theologians are not saying that man has no responsibility, or that he is in no way to be held guilty for the failures
he makes. The emphasis is upon the potentiality; it is not a
backward-looking emphasis upon the mistakes that man can so
easily make.

Another modern theologian of a somewhat different emphasis
is Karl Rahner. His presuppositions are largely Thomist. On
this basis he considers the implication of man's self-existence
and recognizes that the being of man, more than a consideration
of material things, is likely to be a help to our understanding of
being itself. This is not to imply that Rahner is in the old-
fashioned way an idealist who regards matter as unreal. He
recognizes that, in man, mind and spirit co-operate and that
in their co-operation with the divine spirit matter can be
released from its negativity. The body, he says, is not alien to
the spirit but 'a limited factor in the accomplishment of the
spirit itself', or again, 'spirit must be thought of as seeking and
finding itself through the perfection of what is material.'[1] In
other words, spirit is not to be isolated from matter. This is
related to the idea that God is not one among many other
features of our existence, but He is the ground of all existence;
He is known through finite things, and especially through
personal existence.

This idea that man's nature is the most fruitful source of
information about God is also expressed by Moltmann in
Theology of Hope. He argues that both man and God are trans-

---

[1] K. Rahner, *Hominisation*, Burns and Oates, 1965, pp. 58f.

cendent existences, and that they are outside the closed system
of cause and effect. Man, in his self-transcendence, is closest to
the transcendence of God. Rahner expresses something of the
same idea by insisting that the creative activity of God enables
man to transcend himself, and that this transcending himself
means the movement always into a higher realm of being. All this
is a looking-forward to greater possibilities of human nature.
Rahner in this sense is very optimistic. He says: 'the Bible does
not represent man as if all subsequent history were to be regarded
as a decline or at most as a recovery of the original starting
point.' Again, he speaks of 'the inexhaustible plenitude of man's
nature'.[1]

Another modern writer who has illuminated our understanding of the nature of man is David Jenkins, author of *The Glory of
Man*. Jenkins argues that the activity of God is displayed in the
liveliness of man. This seems to be a reference to the extreme
complexity of man's activity, and especially his intellectual
activity—his discovery of new facts and his increasing control
over the world. Here again it is not a matter of setting man
against God but finding the activity of God within the human
race. All these attitudes, which are really only a brief sample of
the sort of things that modern theologians are saying about man,
do seem to me to illustrate the point that modern theology is
becoming far more positive about human nature; and by being
more positive, it is becoming far more constructive in its contribution to modern thinking. It may be, as Altizer says, that
man in our day is realizing that he must be human, that whatever else he is he must be *fully* human, and, if the transcendent
God gets in the way of our humanity, then the transcendent God
must be removed. This must be understood in terms of what I
have already said about the attitude of the 'God is Dead'
theologians. At any rate, I hope the point is reasonably clear
that we can hopefully begin with man; this is not a new assertion of the old humanitarian, or anthropomorphic attitude in
theology, but it does mean that we are now able to combine our
theology with other knowledge, and to look forward to poten-
tentialities and possibilities for man in the future greater than
he has ever known in the past.

How does all this apply to religious education in schools? I

[1] *Hominisation*, Burns and Oates, pp. 105, 109.

am not suggesting that this sort of theological approach which I have briefly outlined can be presented without a great deal of interpretation to children of any age, but I think the implications of what I am saying are very significant for the whole life of the school. If the Christian theologian is prepared to learn the truth about human nature from human sciences, this is really only an illustration of the fact that the Christian is of necessity committed to an appreciation of all knowledge, wherever it is found. Applied in a school situation, it seems to me to mean that the Christian teacher of R.E. is bound to be interested in everything that is being taught in the school. I do not mean he is to interfere or to try to tell other people their business, but rather to see that the Christian view is an integration and an interpretation of all other knowledge. It is not a little bit added on without which the edifice is incomplete, it is an interpretation of all other knowledge as it is learned. It seems to me, then, that Christians should be especially interested in knowledge for its own sake. I suspect that this idea of the intrinsic value of knowledge is rather under a cloud at the moment. There seems to be so much emphasis on learning for the sake of getting a good job and achieving a high status that people easily forget that it is just simply a good thing for man to be educated; indeed, education is essential for the fully human life which it is the aim of Christians to seek for mankind. So what is required of the Christian attitude in this connection is a re-emphasis on the aim of education as the making possible of the fully human life. I emphasize, it is not a matter of the R.E. specialist presuming to interfere in other people's specializations; it is a matter of knowing what the children are learning at every stage and seeking to help them to integrate all this knowledge and to interpret it in terms of a meaningful life.

There is a very long and honourable tradition in the Christian Church of the support of love of learning. Many of the great educational foundations of this country were founded by Christians who were seized by the conviction that learning is necessary for a Christian, necessary for a fully human life. They were concerned to set up organizations in their various institutions which would make true Christian learning possible. In this way I suggest the more hopeful attitude to man may very well be the key to a new optimism in the schools. Not just that we should make R.E. more interesting, although I think through this theological approach this may very well turn out to be the case, but what I am more concerned to emphasize is that through starting again with man, we can help our scholars see that there is a unity and significance and joy in all that they learn and in the whole human life for which they are preparing themselves.

5 | Jesus, Christ, and the New Theology

THE greatest achievement of the new theology is its emphasis upon the centrality of Christ. In order to understand the significance of this emphasis we ought first to notice how this tradition has developed. Liberal Christianity, dominant in British theology at the turn of the century, emphasized the conception of the Jesus of history. There were many lives of Jesus written, and a very attractive picture was painted of him as Lord and Leader. This figure of the human Jesus was very compelling in many of its characteristics and did indeed help many people towards a living faith in Jesus; the human figure was clearly to be seen in the gospel records. His teaching embodied a perfect example which, although belonging to the past, could be applied to the present. The difficulty of this way of looking at Jesus, however, is considerable. The concept of Jesus was inadequate to the total view of his nature revealed in the New Testament; many aspects of the teaching of Jesus, for instance, had to be ignored because they did not fit this figure of a perfect human example whose way was to be followed by modern man. Eschatology (that is, teaching about the destiny of men and the world) for example was almost entirely neglected by this point of view, and along with this inability to face the reality of Jesus' total revelation there went other problems concerning the significance of human need and the problems arising from sin and so on. So that although liberal Christianity was able to communicate very well with its contemporaries, the message it had to convey was in many ways defective and inadequate.

It was the inadequacy and incompleteness of the liberal view of Jesus which produced a violent reaction in the dogmatic theology of Barth, Brunner and Bultmann. These German scholars saw that the significance of Jesus could not be contained within a twentieth-century liberal formula. Account must be taken of those views which did not easily accord with contemporary ideas. The result of this is that eschatology became central to the meaning of the teaching and life of Jesus. This means that the emphasis of this 'Theology of the Word', as it is sometimes called, centred far more upon divine activity. It was not chiefly a consideration of a human example that the Christian message contained, but rather an account of the in-breaking of God into a world in the person of his Son. So the message is about the Kingdom of God, the announcement of its arrival, and the resultant emphasis upon the judgement and power of God; all these conceptions were brought into the centre of thought about Jesus. This was a good emphasis in so far as it restored to the Christian faith a message which was not a mere repetition of contemporary platitudes. But the difficulty of this approach, which has become more apparent as the years have passed, is that it cuts itself off from the contemporary world by its exclusive view of revelation and divine activity. In his early period Barth was violently opposed to any philosophy of religion and to any attempt to see Christianity in the light of other faiths. Christian faith is something which is unique and comes down from God; man must accept it in faith. He cannot hope to reason it out; he cannot reach up to God to find God; all he can do is to accept the truth which is revealed in Jesus. The problem this presents is that, although the message may be very significant and important the communication of it to our contemporaries becomes extremely difficult. The gap between those who hold a religious view of life and those who hold a secular view becomes wider and wider under the influence of this dogmatic theology. The dogmatic emphasis in Christology was far more comprehensive and significant than that of liberal theology, but the difficulty was that the dogmatic emphasis was not communicable to contemporary man.

Before we proceed any further with this discussion it seems necessary that we should attempt some clarification of terminology. For I think that one of the greatest difficulties faced by anyone who is trying to understand what the Christian faith is about is the way in which Christians suddenly begin to talk about 'Christ'. Whom do we mean? Most people can follow us so long as we are talking about a person who once lived, commonly known in his lifetime as Jesus of Nazareth. Even if the claims made for him are not accepted, it is understood that we are talking about a human figure of the past, as we talk of Napoleon, Florence Nightingale, or any other historical figure.

But then we talk about Christ, and it is immediately apparent that we have changed gear; we have altered the universe of discourse. Now we are referring to an alleged 'someone' who does not belong only to the past, but also to the present. We speak of him as someone who is alive; but he cannot be experienced by the senses. He appears to be effective within the normal circumstances of human experience; but the ordinary conditions of human experience do not apply to him.

As far as terminology is concerned, there seems to be much in favour of the distinction being made as follows. Jesus is the man who lived nearly two thousand years ago. Christ is the centre of Christian faith, claimed by many to be known personally; but perhaps by an increasing number regarded not so much in personal terms but as a centre of obligation, conviction and values. A sort of shorthand reference to love, courage, sympathy, concern, peace—indeed all the attitudes which go to make up Christianity.

The difficulty about this distinction is that the terms 'Jesus' and 'Christ' overlap. When we speak of Christ, we are always, I think, implying some reference to Jesus. And it is very difficult for a Christian to think of Jesus simply as a human being and no more. Although I use 'Christ' in a personal sense normally, I do not mean to imply that without this personal sense there is no proper use of the term. I shall try in the following discussion to distinguish the terms as suggested above. 'Jesus' means the historical human being. 'Christ' means the centre of Christian faith, whether personal or impersonal.

The attitude of radical theology to this question of the centrality of Christ is not a compromise between liberalism and dogmatic orthodoxy. Nor is it a revival of either position. The attitude now taken by radical theology on this point is better described as a dialectical development of the former positions. As a result of the questions which have been exercising the mind of Christians for some time, new insights into the position of Christ in theology are becoming apparent. At one extreme, there are some like Altizer to whom theism is no longer tenable. The Incarnation is a development and indeed the end of theism. The meaning of the Incarnation is simply—*God is Jesus*. This, of course, is an extreme position and in itself may indeed be untenable. It is the extreme emphasis upon the centrality of Jesus which has given rise to the not altogether unreasonable comment that to the new theologians there is no God and Jesus is his Son!

Nevertheless, the new theology approach to the question of the meaning of Jesus does reveal new insights and new possibilities of understanding, and especially we now begin to see the problem of the person of Christ from a different viewpoint. Formerly, it seemed as if the problem could be put in this form. How can God, whom we know, and man, whom also we know, be found together in one unified coherent personality? That is, how can so different realities as we know God and man to be combine together in one incarnate person? The assumption behind this way of approaching the question of the person of Christ is, you will notice, that we already know God and we already know man. The problem then is how can we conceive of their unification? More and more modern theology tends to see the question in a different form. The problem really is, do we know enough about God or about man to be able to conceive of conditions of their unification, apart from the Incarnation? The Incarnation is now seen to be a means whereby we see the truth about God and the truth about man, and it is very significant that these truths are found together and therefore must not be taken apart. We cannot draw conclusions about God from Jesus and proceed to understand these truths in separation from their original context. God cannot be known apart from man, and equally man cannot be known apart from God.

So modern theology is thoroughly Christocentric. There are no theological questions that can be properly asked, let alone answered, apart from Christ. This is the cumulative result of a development of Christological emphasis which certainly owes a great deal to the work of the dogmatic theologians and to the earlier work of the liberal Christians. Modern theology directs our attention to Christ, and this I would say is one of its greatest benefits. It is indeed so great a benefit as to outweigh any loss that may be felt regarding its minimizing and reducing tendency. But at the same time this very emphasis on Christ raises a most critical issue for modern theology. If modern theology insists that the whole Christian faith centres upon Christ, the question immediately arises, what if this supposed centre is not knowable? Do we have enough knowledge about the historical basis of the gospels to be able to base upon this a full Christian doctrine? Would it be fair to say, as the cynics seem to be saying, that Christianity is centred upon Christ, but that when full investigation is made of Christ we find there is no substance there; that Christianity appears to have a hollow centre? This is in my view one of the most central questions being raised by theology today.

The first part of the question is about historicity. Has the form critic destroyed our confidence in the historical figure to the extent that we can no longer really say anything definite about Jesus? Some accept this position, and reply that it doesn't really matter because we have the Christ of faith and this is adequate to our need. But this total abandonment of historicity is of course a position open to very great difficulties. It does really mean an almost complete abandoning of the whole of the New Testament, not only the Gospels; and also a complete break from traditional Christianity. For traditional Christianity has always been concerned about a historical person in the centre of faith. Admittedly this concern has not always expressed itself in the emphasis on literal history which has been dominant over the last hundred years in Western Christendom, but the idea of a historical manifestation in the person of Jesus is so central to the Christian tradition that to remove it is to challenge that tradition in its most vital part. A further difficulty of this 'Christ of faith, never mind about the historical person' attitude is that it is very difficult to see how such a view can be distinguished from pious imagination. How do we know that a person or idea we talk about as 'the Christ of faith' is any more than something just made up to suit our own ends?

Faced with this apparent destruction of the basis of faith, some have reacted very violently against form criticism and all its works, and have regarded it as of the devil. Perhaps it is hardly necessary to say that it is no valid reason to reject a method of study just because the results are unpleasant and unwelcome. If form criticism is to be criticized it must be on the basis of its methods and assumptions, not because we don't like its results. The view taken in this book is that the assumptions and methods of form criticism are basically sound, and we must therefore resolutely face the consequences. This does admittedly involve a real risk to faith, but this is preferable to a faith which is afraid of facing the consequences of truth, whatever they may be.

But in fact form criticism does *not* leave us without a basis for the concept of a historical person of Jesus. This is not only, or chiefly, because form criticism accepts some historical basis for the story of Jesus; it is even more because through these memories and traditions we are given a clear portrait of a person upon whom our faith rests. It does need to be said again and again that it is no part of the result of the form critical attitude to suppose that Christians were making up an idealized figure as the centre of faith. This was not done in the first century. The early Church did not make up a figure according to its own imagination and it has never done so since. There is an objectivity and centrality about the person of Jesus which is the guide and rule of the life of faith.

For instance, it is evident that the Christians of the first century did not merely read into the life of Jesus their own concept of faith. It is valuable to notice the difference of emphasis between the faith of the first Christians and their presentation of the person of Christ. They show us in the gospels one who calls men to faith in God; but the Church through which this faith is transmitted spoke equally of faith in God and in Christ. Again, the early Church, under the leadership of St Paul, had a very severe doctrine of sin; the view of sin presented in the teaching of Jesus is far less severe than the Pauline view. The Holy Spirit is a central and extremely important concept in the thought of the early Church, but in the gospels the Spirit has a comparatively minor role. In the gospels there is no reference to the Spirit producing in believers the life of Christ and the fruits of the Spirit. There is, then, good ground for saying that the early Church has not presented an idealized figure; it has, in fact, presented a figure based upon a clear tradition and a very discernible person comes through the portrait they present.

This portrait is presented not only in the gospels but also in the rest of the New Testament. It is important to recognize, for instance, that in the Epistle to the Hebrews we have a clear outline of a person in whom suffering, obedience and humility are the clearest and strongest characteristics. In other words, it is wrong to try to isolate the Jesus presented in the gospels and claim that this alone is the authentic historical person; one of the most valuable results of form criticism is to enable us to see not only in straightforward historical accounts, but also in the accounts of the faith and experience of the early Church, a portrait of this person who is the centre of the faith. This portrait is absolutely vital to the Christian faith today. Unless our faith is securely anchored to the facts of the historic Incarnation, which refer not only to a person who lived but also to the effect of this person on other people; unless this is the centre of our faith, how can we avoid the suspicion that all our religious talk is mere pious imagination?

This religious talk is not fully comprehended in terms of a person who lived a long time ago and is remembered a long time after. To many people the greatest offence of Christian talk about Christ is that it assumes that this Christ is alive; that the person who lived and died rose again and still lives in the world. He it is to whom the Christian faith bears witness. He is the central reality of the Christian faith and to him new theology is bearing an impressive witness. This witness is still significant even when there is hesitation to ascribe personal terms to it. Sometimes this impressive witness is put in the extreme form of saying we can no longer believe in God; we can believe in Christ but not in God. This is a position which needs careful examination. The assumption seems to be that it is easier to believe in Christ than it is to believe in God. Certainly it seems more attractive, for Christ seems to be a more real and approachable person than the distant majestic figure of God. But as we have already seen in our discussion of form criticism, it is dangerous to base belief on what seems attractive or unattractive to us. Have we in fact any more reason for believing in Christ than we have for believing in God?

In terms of the problem of verification, believing in Christ seems to be as difficult as believing in God. How do we verify or falsify statements about Christ? It is true that there are possibly empirical verifications concerning the life of Jesus of Nazareth, but this is not really the point that is being raised. The point upon which we seek verification or falsification is about statements concerning Christ, which involve much more than statements about a historical person of long ago. How do we know, for instance, that Jesus and Christ are the same person? Unless we can make sure of this, any verification about Jesus is not necessarily a verification about Christ.

To put it another way, there seems to be a greater problem about proving the existence of Christ than there is even about proving the existence of God. We may be dissatisfied with the arguments about the existence of God, yet the theistic proofs do seem to come very near to cumulative evidence that there is likely to be a God. Some theologians suggest that even though these arguments cannot stand alone, the questions they raise about the idea of God and the incredibility of an accidental universe do support the theistic claim. Further, there seem to be some grounds for supposing that a new-style natural theology may be able to find even greater value in some of these old arguments for the existence of God. But what similar or equal arguments are there for the existence of Christ? No one even suggests that the reality of Christ can be proved or demonstrated by this sort of argument. The argument isn't even there to be knocked down. This is even more obvious when we think in terms of the effects of God's activity. If we can allow the possibility of the existence of God, then by definition his activity will be seen in creation; in the development of a good life for man; in the growth of knowledge and in the order of the natural world. But there seems to be no possible similar conclusion that can be drawn about the existence of Christ; if Christ exists then what would be the conclusions which it would be natural to draw? The answer to this question seems to be extremely difficult.

Why then do we believe in Christ? How can we answer those who are mystified and can only think that we are self-deluded when we talk about this 'person' who is the centre of the Christian faith? The answer that a Christian gives to this question seems to have two bases—tradition and experience. It is not without significance that both these categories are generally out of favour among us today. A generation which despises tradition and doubts the validity of experience is not likely to find it easy to believe in Christ. Nevertheless these are the foundations of the Christian faith, and they must be expounded in a way which will make them acceptable to our contemporaries.

Tradition begins with the apostles' awareness of the fact of the Resurrection. There is no need to exempt the Resurrection appearances from the close scrutiny which we apply to all other parts of the gospels. Indeed, it is natural to regard them as mythical expressions of the convictions of different people in different circumstances that Jesus was alive. This means that questions about the reality of the empty tomb and whether this can ever be empirically verified, and questions about what was this half-spiritual, half-physical entity with which the disciples were in contact can be misleading. Questions about the place and time of the ascension must be related to the fact that there is more than one tradition about this—the gospel of Luke, for instance, implying that the ascension took place on the day of Resurrection, and the Acts of the Apostles implying that it took place forty days after the Resurrection. All these questions are important in themselves but do not go to the real heart of the issue. The real issue of the Resurrection appearances is that they are statements that Christ is alive. The central significance of this is that the statement that Christ is alive is made by people who had good reason to be sceptical and were in a uniquely favourable position to know whether they were truly in contact with the same entity they had known in the flesh. They say Christ is alive and they identify Christ with Jesus. Here history and experience are uniquely fused and made accessible to human awareness.

But why should we believe them? After all, it is the universal experience of mankind that dead men don't live again. Why should we throw aside all human experience to believe this? The answer to this very relevant and proper question is that these men's lives and subsequent events confirm the profession

they make. Their lives were consistent with their claims. The
result of their witness is there for all to see. Not even the most
fervent cynic can deny that within three hundred years this
hopeless band of not very gifted men had won official recognition in the empire. Of course, it could be a colossal confidence
trick, but if you believe that you are surely credulous to an
alarming degree.

And this conviction that Christ is alive has a remarkable
survival value. It has taken hold of men of widely different
ability and culture—often leading them into positions they
would never choose and from which in all ordinary circumstances they would shrink. This conviction that Christ is alive
has a wonderful power of self-criticism and renewal. It has
often been held by people whose lives ought to have finished it
off for ever, since they and we have been such blatant contradictions of what is being professed. There is continuity and adapta-
bility in the Christian faith, evidenced throughout the ages,
which it is not unreasonable to credit to the truth of what
Christians claim: that is, that Christ is alive.

The other basis for belief in Christ's reality is experience.
This is very widely criticized by our contemporaries on the
grounds that it is impossible, from the basis of experience, to
demonstrate the reality of any external fact. So that while our
critics will not deny that we have experience, they will deny
that it is an experience of Christ. They say it is impossible for
anyone to say that Christ is alive just because he has an experience of him. All he has is an experience. But this argument
is not really meeting the claim that a Christian makes in this
connection. The awareness of Christ involves the necessity of an
external reality, for Christian experience is not just an awareness; it is awareness of Christ. If you take away the reality of
Christ, supposing you could, you don't leave behind an awareness of something vague; you leave behind nothing at all. Its no
use telling a Christian believer that he is entitled to claim an
experience but not a reality, because for him the experience and
reality are one.

This experience is very difficult to describe because it is so
varied. It involves feeling, but not equally all the time, and it
is not exclusively feeling. It is sometimes evoked by reading the
Bible, sometimes by worship, especially sacramental worship,

sometimes by association with other Christians, and sometimes it seems to arise from nowhere at all. It has certain distinguishable common features in its normal manifestation. These include a sense of purpose not known before; a solution to many personal problems, especially those problems which arise out of personal failure; a desire to improve the quality of one's life, a tendency to join together with others who have the same desires and convictions; and most of all, a desire to worship God and to serve one's fellow men.

When people in different ages and different countries with different cultural backgrounds all say that these things are an experience of Christ, attention must be given to their claim. It is true that the onset of this awareness remains a mystery, and today there are peculiar problems facing those who are interested in these claims but cannot find them real for themselves. Past experience in the Church, however, reminds us that this awareness has a great power of adaptation, and it is often true that the faith which is most difficult to find is the one which in the end is most effective.

So if Christ is the centre of the Christian faith we may hazard some answer to the question 'What is the content of this awareness and how can it be justified as real and not imaginary?' But the question remains as to the significance of Christ for us today. If we can, as we have argued, affirm the reality of Christ, how can we clarify what Christ is for us today? I have already hinted that religious talk in this area is extremely confusing to those who are not in the closed circle of believers, and this is even more true for children. Children tend to objectify all their convictions and they find it extremely difficult to understand what is meant by this unseen, unheard, non-empirical reality whom Christians call Christ.

It is not difficult to appreciate that 'Jesus' is a human name, attractive in its humanity and for that reason used all the more for the central figure of the Christian faith. Perhaps at this point it is not out of place to remind ourselves that in the past a tendency to allow the Christian faith to degenerate into a 'Jesus cult' has proved very unfortunate. There is the same danger today which must be carefully avoided. The Christian faith must not degenerate into hero-worship. The term 'Christ' is more difficult to clarify because its status usually seems to hover between a personal and a family name. No doubt for many grown-ups as well as for children, 'Jesus Christ' seems exactly parallel to 'John Smith'. In this case Christ would be, of course, a surname. The fact is that the term Christ is a Jewish title linking our Lord with the continuing revelation of God—in the Old Testament and the New. There is a good theological point in this idea of continuous revelation, but what does the name mean to twentieth-century Christians? I suppose it has become a recognized title having rather more implication of the present living reality of God than has the term 'Jesus'. But there is in my view an unfortunate tendency in modern theology to limit talk about Jesus Christ to the term Jesus when reference is being made to his present reality, so that very often the question is asked 'What is Jesus for us today?' I would prefer to retain the traditional 'Jesus Christ' title, for this has wide implications about the humanity and also the living present reality of Christ.

Still the question remains, what is Jesus Christ for us today? Modern theologians seem very attracted to the title 'Jesus is Lord'. (To use my suggested terminology strictly, this should be 'Christ is Lord'. But the phrase is too well established to be altered.) In some ways this attraction is very strange in these democratic days and maybe we ought to point out that strictly speaking to say 'Jesus is Lord' is no more conformable to present day ideas than to say 'Jesus is King', or 'Jesus is Saviour'. Nevertheless it is a title which has attracted great attention. It has a very early authentication in the New Testament and it does seem full of potential meaning, especially when we allow for proper demythologizing of it in the twentieth century.

For one thing, the title 'Jesus is Lord' can refer to the total rule of God exercised through Christ over the whole universe. This is an important feature of the Christian faith. The Christian faith is not content to think of God only in terms of personal relation with the individual believer. The Christian faith includes the conviction that God is ruling over all things; the implication of this conviction raises questions about God's providential rule and divine care and we shall later be considering these questions, but it is certainly true that in saying 'Jesus is Lord' we are expressing our confidence in the order of things and the conviction that in Christ we have the clue to the meaning of the universe.

'Jesus is Lord' is also a confession of personal obedience. It is an assertion that we have taken up the position of obedience to our Lord's commands. The application of this obedience to practical affairs is a continual challenge to Christian living. We do well to remind ourselves that it is little use talking about the overruling authority of God over all creation if we ourselves are not willing to be obedient to God in our own affairs and our own responsibilities. The obedience of the Christian, therefore, is greatly emphasized in the concept Jesus is Lord, and this no doubt is why the term is so attractive to many modern thinkers. The working-out of this obedience requires consultation with our fellow Christians. It requires a continual awareness of what the present day issues really are, and a continual sensitiveness to the meaning of Christ for today. This can only be gained by openness to the revelation of Christ through scripture and Christian worship.

One aspect of this obedience which is especially significant in our time is the way in which this obedience to Christ will lead to a fuller human life for those who accept the obedience, and through them for those whom they serve. We are learning not only from theology but also from contemporary secular thinking that the aim of God's salvation is that we should live a fully human life. When we are living a fully human life we have found what Christ is for us today. This is one of the most significant implications of the concept of the presence of Christ in human life; it is at the same time an illumination of the meaning of humanity in terms of the relation between God and man.

When we consider how the attitude outlined in this chapter can be applied in the teaching of religion in schools, the first issue seems to me to be, 'How can we use the form critical approach to the New Testament?' Generally speaking our assumption seems to be that we can first of all teach the New Testament in more or less historical terms and only later need we raise the questions about the possible influence of the faith of the Church upon the records of the life of Jesus. I suggest that much more thought should be given to the way in which our approach to the gospels and the story of Jesus right from the beginning should be an approach of faith. In my view it is a mistake first of all to present Jesus as the centre of a hero-cult and then later try to superimpose upon this the conception of the Christ in whom we believe. I am convinced that children are quite capable of realizing the significance for today of what it means to believe in Christ. We only create difficulties for them by trying to speak firstly of the person of the past about whom these stories are told and whose example we are supposed to follow. Why can we not all the time present the picture of Christ as a living present Lord whose portrait is given to us in the New Testament? If we were to approach it this way it seems to me that many of the subsequent difficulties would be met much more satisfactorily. There would be no need for children to make the big jump between thinking about someone who lived a long time ago and then trying to connect this with someone who lives now in the reality of the Christian faith.

There is also the question as to what extent this approach can be criticized as being indoctrination rather than teaching. This criticism may mean to imply that it is all right to talk about past events in a historical or literary sense, but it is not all right to talk about Christ in contemporary terms of faith and obedience. If this is the issue, then to accept the charge of indoctrination means that we can no longer continue to teach the Christian faith, for the Christian faith is not simply a matter of historical fact. It is a matter of a belief about the meaning of life; about the presence of Christ and obedience to that presence. I do not see how we can teach the Christian faith effectively without presenting a Lord in whom we believe, in whom we hope the children will believe. I am sure there is very little point in just teaching the facts—meaning the historical and literary facts about the life of Jesus—if no attempt is made to encourage a response to this person who is being talked about; a response which will lead to Christian faith. In this sense there is not that stark difference between teaching and preaching that some people have often supposed; preaching involves a statement of fact with view to a verdict; and teaching also involves the presentation of a case, a presentation in such a way as we hope will make it commendable and acceptable to the people whom we teach.

There is real point in the suspicion of indoctrination when only a selection of facts are presented, a selection which is strongly biased towards one point of view. In the past this was the ground of the suspicion of denominational schools. Non-Anglicans were especially sensitive to the possibility that only Anglican doctrine would be taught in schools dominated by religious motives. It is well to remember that this was the reason for the agreed syllabuses. If today we find these increasingly unsuitable for our purposes, we should remember that they were designed to ensure that religious teaching was given to every child, and that the teaching should not be indoctrination by any particular denomination.

The situation today is different. There is practically no danger that denominational bias will influence our teaching. But many do say that Religious Education is too confessional. It is only the Christian point of view that is taught. Other world faiths have come much nearer to us because of immigration, and also there has been a considerable growth of Humanism among our contemporaries. So, it is argued, these views should be given equal prominence with Christianity.

It must be allowed by any fair-minded person that there is much substance in this argument. It does seem unreasonable that children should not be told anything about non-Christian religious views, and be given no opportunity to choose for themselves which attitude to life they will adopt. Of course, the position is not as bad as many critics make out. In many schools a good deal is taught about non-Christian religions, and most schools have members of staff who are well able to propagate humanist ideas, and who do not hesitate to do so. But it is surely necessary that this process of widening the range of religious instruction should be accelerated, and given more official support. This is not only common fairness. Without this reference to other religions, students will increasingly resent what appears to them to be a deliberate attempt to keep information from them. We all know that forbidden information is most eagerly sought. If the information is not given accurately in school it will be assimilated in a garbled version out of school, resulting in much prejudice and ignorance of other people's convictions.

A word of warning may not be out of place. By all means let

us widen our syllabuses to include Humanism and non-Christian religions. The danger is that we spread the subject so widely that we end up with a very thin layer of syncretism, which proves inadequate as a basis for living. It is very difficult to give a fair account of a religion which we do not personally embrace. This applies to Christians teaching Buddhism or Hinduism just as much as to Humanists teaching Christianity. Christians who attempt to give an account of the Muslim faith should try to imagine how they would react in a Mohammedan country if children were 'taught' Christianity by a Muslim in a few short lessons. It is possibly better to concentrate comparative study of religion on one or two non-Christian faiths, which are specially relevant because of a multi-racial situation, rather than to try to cover all the world religions in the time at our disposal.

And the background must still be, for us, an open and enlightened exposition of the Christian faith. We are not in the job for polemical purposes; but we ought to be able to explain the basis of our convictions, and present them in as persuasive a form as possible. We have to accept the possibility that new insights into the perennial problems with which religion deals will arise from non-Christian sources. There is no need for a convinced Christian to fear such a possibility, for in every world religion there must be much truth, or it would never have survived. Only the person who thinks that he has truth nicely sewn up in a packet will be afraid of new insights arising from many different sources.

6 | *What can we say about God?*

WE NOW come to the biggest question of all. Is there anything that can now be said about God when we take into account the difficulties which appear in connection with belief in our present situation? It is obvious that there have always been problems connected with speaking about God to children. The apparent ease of speaking of God as Father always runs into the difficulty of what the concept of 'Father' means to children. There is the further difficulty that children are inevitably taking the idea of 'Father' in the sense of an external person and this leads to great difficulties about the concept of God in later years. A further comment on this contemporary situation is that other ideas connected with God are also now seen to be under serious question. For instance, when God is regarded as the cause and explanation of everything, this seems a very convenient way of encouraging faith in and dependence upon God. But children should be encouraged to realize that all natural phenomena are, at any rate in theory, explicable in natural terms. Their experience confirms that we have to depend very largely on our own efforts. Thus the concept of God as explanation and universal provider is no longer tenable. The problem here is twofold. On the one hand we have to consider what we can in honesty and sincerity say about God. It is no use speaking about God to children in a way which is not genuine, for children sooner than adults are able to detect insincerity. But the other problem is what can now be said about God which can be understood by children? Is it possible to talk about God in non-substantial, maybe non-personal terms, in a way which children will understand? Here we face almost insoluble problems but it is in this area that our thinking must be directed. We have to find ways whereby the post-substantial view of God such as we have been hinting at can be made meaningful to children. In order to attempt this task we shall first look at some of the ways in which modern thinkers are trying to state views of God which are not susceptible to the criticism that they are too objective or too substantial.

It is a great mistake to think that all modern theologians are saying that God is dead. Many modern thinkers speak about God in other ways which avoid the open and apparent atheism of that particular expression. But, in fact, in several cases their position comes to the same thing. For instance, R. B. Braithwaite, in *An Empiricist's View of Religion*, says that statements about God are really statements about morals. That is, when we say God is love, we are not really saying anything about a supposed external reality. We are really saying that we believe that love is the way to live; we are committing ourselves (to use Braithwaite's terminology) to an 'agapeistic' way of life. In this way Braithwaite claims that religious language can still be employed, although he recognizes that it is not really being used in the traditional way. Another thinker who takes a similar point of view is T. R. Miles in *Religion and the Scientific Attitude*. Miles says that statements about God can only be made in the form of what he calls theistic parables. That is, when we are talking about God we are using the form of the parable in a similar way to that in which Jesus used parables to illustrate his meaning. For example, 'A certain man went down from Jerusalem to Jericho and fell among thieves'. Now if anyone asks of that parable, what was the man's name, or why was he going to Jericho, or what time of year was it when he made the journey, we all realize that he is asking questions which have no relevance. It doesn't matter what the man's name was or why he was going or what time of the year it was. The parable is a way of expressing a truth in the form of a story. The truth does not depend on the literal details of the story. In the same way, argues Miles, talk about God is not to be taken in a literalistic way. It is to be taken as a means of expressing truths which cannot be expressed in any other way. This means that when we speak about God we are not really referring to an external entity at all; we are referring to the religious conviction which does not, he claims, depend on belief in such a person outside human life. Paul van Buren, in *The Secular Meaning of the Gospel*, takes a similar line in which he rejects entirely all ideas of supernaturalism. Van Buren is greatly influenced by linguistic philosophy and is sensitive to the criticism that statements about an external entity look like empirical statements but in fact have no discernible means of empirical verification or falsification. So the statements which faith makes must not be taken to refer to any supernatural entity and he comes to more or less the same conclusion as Braithwaite and Miles.

The difficulty about these three typical attempts to speak of God without really referring to an external reality is that in each case the language seems to have been radically changed in meaning. The effect of this is that once such a change is accepted and realized one wonders whether the former religious statements will continue to be made. Once we are convinced that speaking about 'God is love' is really speaking about what we intend to do; and talking about God's activity is really talking in terms of parables which are not meant factually, I think most people will cease to use this sort of language. Its meaning has been so radically changed that the language itself becomes redundant. This, I think, is the truth in the assertion that these thinkers are just as atheistic as the 'God is dead' theologians. They do not put it in such clear and challenging form, but in fact they are really retreating from the field. They are retaining the language but the substance of the language has been abandoned. One cannot suppose that this is a satisfactory way of speaking about God.

In order to find a more satisfactory answer to the question of what we can say about God, we have to look beyond the immediate contemporary generation of theologians to an earlier generation.

Paul Tillich has rightly been regarded as one of the formative thinkers behind the new theology. His theological position is notoriously difficult to understand and even more difficult to summarize. It is as well to realize that it is a very difficult matter to break into Tillich's theology at any point and hope to make sense of what he is trying to say. One of the important features of his theology is that it is a system which must be taken as a whole. Nevertheless, at the risk of misunderstanding what Tillich has said, I think we have to try to say something about his 'theology of being'. One must remember that Tillich's attitude is existential in the sense that he thinks that theology not only originates in the self-conscious being of man, but also must be applied in an actual living human situation. This means that the very difficult question of the significance of being has to be understood. One of the most searching questions that we can ask of our existence is, why should it be at all? Indeed, why should anything be at all? When we consider the nature of the being of man we find that characteristically this being expresses itself in a life of individual freedom. The most significant characteristic of this being is its difference from the being of things. The clear differentiation between the existence of people and the existence of things is of course one of the fundamental conceptions of existentialism. When we consider the nature of human existence, we find that it is not only individual and seeking to be free, but it is also an existence filled with anxiety and fear and insecurity. These attitudes, says Tillich, arise from 'a profound and desperate feeling of meaninglessness'.[1] As we shall see later, other theologians have taken up this notion that through consideration of the existence of the self, rather than of the existence of things, we can more readily understand what we mean by the reality of God. But for the moment let us continue with the view of Tillich. He is prepared to say that God does not exist. This is not to say there is no God. It is asserting that existence applies to human being, not to divine being. Tillich asserts that the meaning of God is that which underlies the being of man. This is what he means by speaking of God as 'the ground of being'. This implies that when we speak of God we are speaking of that which is a necessary pre-requisite and implication of our own existence. Another valuable insight that Tillich gives us is that this ground of being is closely related to what is our ultimate concern. God is that which deeply and ultimately concerns us. God is not a being outside human situations on whom we can call for help. He is one upon whom our whole being rests.

[1] Paul Tillich, *Systematic Theology*, Vol. 1, p. 223.

This idea of God understood in terms of being rather than in terms of substance, difficult though it is, seems to open up the way to a new understanding of God for our time. There are two particular developments of this conception to which I want to draw attention. Firstly, as John Macquarrie says,[1] the nature of being is, in terms of Christian faith, 'holy' being. In other words, the distinctive characteristic of the man of faith is not that he believes in being. One cannot very well do other than believe in being, seeing that it is a conception that underlies all reality. But the attitude of faith is that being is holy. A further characteristic of this holy being to which Macquarrie draws attention is its function of 'letting be', as he calls it. By this he means that holy being is that which continually causes other beings to exist. Its function is especially creative and formative.

Another characteristic of being which has been emphasized by some modern thinkers is equally important. This is that being is encountered and understood best in the nature of our own being. Karl Rahner, for instance, argues that the Christian attitude to God develops from the consideration of what is meant by the self-existent. Self-existence involves a degree of transcendence. There is always more to the existence of the human being than can be expressed. We all have some awareness of the way in which our experiences transcend, that is, go beyond our powers of expression. We all know that there are dreams and aims and ideals which are part of our human nature which can only reach fulfilment outside the limitations of life as we know it. This is what is meant by referring to human nature as self-transcendent. On the basis of this understanding we can more readily appreciate what is meant by the transcendence of God. This is not to be understood at all in spatial terms but in terms of that which goes beyond and which exceeds the bounds of experience as it is known. One of the chief issues facing Christian theology today is, in what sense can the transcendence of God still be maintained? It seems that in this idea of the meaning of transcendence applied to self-existence there may be a clue to a better understanding of divine transcendence. At any rate, many modern theologians are very far from abandoning the concept of transcendence.

[1] *Principles of Christian Theology*, S.C.M. Press, Ch. V.

They recognize that however inadequate the language may be, it is still necessary for Christians to realize that they are believing in God who is both within human experience and beyond human experience.

This leads to another most interesting development of this approach to the nature of God. It will not have escaped notice that again and again the problem of the traditional view of God is that it is mostly related to the peripheral situations of life. It is when man is unable to cope that he calls in this external God to help him. Thus it is often man's weakness or lack of understanding which gives rise to the concept of God. We all realize the difficulty that this approach creates. More and more the situations in which man is not able to cope are being reduced in significance. As man understands more and more of his situation, he seems to need God less and less. Yet at the same time religious faith seems to be essential to the full meaning of life. The answer that this type of theology which we are now considering gives to this question is that we are to expect to encounter God not only in the peripheral situations but in the central and normal situations of human existence. This means that in our ordinary activities and not only in so-called religious activity, we can expect to come face to face with God. This indeed is what many people are finding today. No doubt this raises many problems about the significance and importance of Christian worship with which we ought to deal in our consideration of worship in school. But it is a great mistake to think that the only situations in which we can meet God are those in which we set up a deliberately religious atmosphere and, so to speak, 'turn on' religion. Rather, in all our learning, in all our experience, in all our activity, there is the possibility that we shall meet God and he will make himself known to us. In the theology of being there is not only some alternative to the idea that God is dead but, what is far more important, there is the possibility of a real religious attitude on the basis of the idea of being.

Another approach to the question of a modern understanding of the meaning of God is being developed through what is known as 'process theology'. Process theology is based on the philosophical system of A. N. Whitehead. One of the most interesting features of this philosophy is its restatement of a metaphysical viewpoint. Metaphysics is the study of the nature of reality; by its very character it assumes the possibility of a coherent unified view—'a coherent, logical, necessary system of general ideas in terms of which every element of our experience can be interpreted'.[1] The metaphysical system developed by Whitehead takes into account modern scientific theories such as relativity and quantum physics, and expresses a view of reality arising out of the inter-relation of entities. That which is real is continually in process, affecting and being affected by other entities through what Whitehead calls 'prehension'. This theory also means that every entity is 'transcended'—that is, it cannot be totally understood in terms of itself alone, but only by reference to that which is 'outside' it.

Whitehead never came to a firm conclusion about belief in God, but it is obvious that his philosophical system certainly makes belief in God tenable, and indeed the system really requires the postulate of God as its basis. But the more important implication of Whitehead's philosophy is that it enables us to think of God in terms of the process of becoming—which is the meaning of all entities. Thus God is not separated from the world of things by the barrier of unchangeability and non-temporality. Rather God can be regarded as so involved in the process of reality that he is deeply affected by what happens to the world. This opens up a far more satisfactory view of the love of God, which Whitehead asserts to be the fundamental contribution of Christianity to thought about God. The love of God for man cannot be one-sided; it must involve sharing man's sorrow and despair. If this comes into conflict with the concept of the 'impassibility' or the 'omnipotence' of God, then these concepts must be either abandoned or restated in the light of God's love. This idea of the love of God inevitably involving God in pain and sorrow is closely linked with the view of salvation which I discuss in Chapter VII.

Another aspect of this philosophy of process is the emphasis it places on freedom. All entities, including apparently totally physical ones, have an element of mind, which is expressed in some degree of freedom. Out of this freedom suffering arises for man, since the universe has a certain chance element which on occasion causes unpleasant and even disastrous effects. Ulti-

[1] A. N. Whitehead.

mately the answer to this problem of suffering, at least in terms of explanation, must be found in accepting the world as it is. To say suffering ought not to be is to say this universe ought not to be as it is—and this is in effect saying it ought not to be at all.

The idea that all entities affect each other through mutual prehension gives some insight into prayer, No longer is the problem how can we explain that God is influenced by our petition, nor how can he be conceived as affecting the course of events. This old problem arose because God was regarded as separate and completely distinct from the world. Any influence from God upon the natural world seemed to imply that God would sometimes, in special cases, interfere in the normal course of nature. But, it was urged, God does not interfere in the ordered process of nature—indeed some have argued that God not only would not, but could not, since he had given up the possibility of doing so by virtue of creating a law-abiding universe. Now if, as the process philosophers say, all events are inter-related, and if reality is a process of becoming, there is nothing unusual in events being influenced by other events— indeed, this is the normal state of affairs. The idea of man's prayers influencing the course of events is not based upon an exception to the general rule of a closed universe but rather is an expression of a basic condition of the inter-related universe. And this means that not only our prayers, but also everything else that we are and do, have their effect upon the subsequent course of events. Every action we take, every decision we make, every thought which passes through our minds, has its effect on the universe. So prayer is not a contracting out of the ordinary sequence, and asking for 'interference' from God. It is obeying the rules of prehension and interaction.

Notice, too, that this view means that God himself is affected by what men do as well as by the prayers they offer. Process theology takes us a long way from the notion that God remains unmoved in his exalted majesty, quite unaffected by our comings and goings, our successes and failures. On the contrary, everything that happens in the world has its effect on God. When one comes to think of it this way, the argument is surely irresistible. For if God really loves us, and if we are using love in anything like the same sense as when we talk about human love, then we are bound to say that in his love for men God is influenced by what men do; he cannot remain indifferent to men's situations. And this seems to me to lead straight into the meaning of the Incarnation. When the God-man appeared, this was not the first time that God had shown an interest in the world. On the contrary, it is a particular and most significant expression of the truth that has always been true—that in his love, God is involved in all that goes on in the world.

Thus a view of God in terms of process philosophy, so unpromising to a generation which regards metaphysics as the heaviest encumbrance theology has to carry, turns out to provide valuable insights into the meaning of God for modern man. It also provides a useful counter weight to those theologians who want to evacuate theology of all objective statements about God. Instead of acquiescing in the view that theological statements can only be about human feelings, intentions, or convictions, the process theologians such as Charles Hartshorne are saying that we must still talk about God. And what is far more important, we must still talk *to* God. Process theology emphasises that worship and prayer are essential to belief in God—a point much needing emphasis in an age which has excelled many others in its ability to express its ideas about God, whether in negative or positive fashion, but which has been singularly deficient in nurturing a relation with God without which all God-talk is really vacuous.

Whitehead's philosophy is undoubtedly difficult and sometimes obscure. It is not the only tenable philosophy for modern man; indeed, until quite recently, it has been almost totally neglected by professional philosophers. Christian theology must beware of tying itself too closely to the apron strings of any philosophy. But Schubert Ogden is surely right in saying about process philosophy, 'No contemporary philosophy is nearly so well qualified to integrate the cumulative insights of the whole western philosophical tradition, so as to do justice to the legitimate motives both of classical metaphysics and of the various forms of modern critical philosophy.'[1] Equally, the theology built upon it is not the whole truth or the final answer. But it does open up new possibilities of a metaphysical basis for theology, without which theology is doomed to wither and die.

In the theology of being and in process theology we have two

[1] *The Reality of God*, S.C.M. Press, pp. 95f.

modern attempts to restate the meaning of God. Their importance lies not so much in any conclusive dogma they may produce as in the fact that both employ ideas which are of central
importance to modern thought. Existentialism, upon which the
theology of being is based, gives expression to our conviction that
human life is uniquely significant. Process thought recalls us to
some of the big questions about the meaning and unity of all
reality, which the mind of man has never been able to ignore
for very long. But at the same time these two concepts seem to
present insuperable difficulties when we try to communicate
them to children. Perhaps the old substantial ideas were decep-
tively easy to make understandable. But how can we possibly
begin to talk to children in terms of 'being' and 'process'? This is
the real problem that new theology presents to the teacher. It's
all very well to say that old ideas of God must go; but what have
we to suggest about presenting new ideas in a way that has any
chance of being understood?

The problem is so severe that it is natural for many to think
that the best way forward is to go back to the Bible. The
attraction of this is increased when we realize that in the teaching of Jesus concrete personal terms such as father, judge, king,
property owner (lord of the vineyard, husbandman, etc.), are
used, and these are much more attractive and understandable
than philosophical words like being and process. It is no part
of the work of a theologian to create stumbling blocks for
unwary feet, and the vivid personal expressions of the gospels
will always be a source of great enlightenment and encouragement to us. Yet we do need to realize that all these terms are
symbols. We have an almost unavoidable tendency to turn
symbols into literal expressions; we objectify our symbols, and
create for ourselves problems about the objectivity of God which
Christian theology has always tried to avoid.

If the names applied to God in the gospels are symbols, which
are not be taken literally, what use can we make of them? Many
people look upon demythologizing as irreverent or presump-
tuous, especially if it is applied to such expressions as the Fatherhood of God. Yet providing we remember that symbols are
never mere symbols, that they always mean something, something which must be expressed in suitable contemporary terms,
then we need have no fear about demythologizing the names of

God. Indeed, even with 'Father', which is the most popular name of God in use today, everyone does demythologize it to some extent. No one really thinks that the Fatherhood of God means exactly the same as human fatherhood. Only in a very oblique way does it refer to generation; it does not include the discovery common to all experiences of human parenthood, that fathers are not infallible, that they grow old and die. We do not really use 'Father' of God in a literal sense. All the demythologizing approach does is to pursue the process further along the same lines.

The question then is, what is the reality behind the symbol? In the case of our Lord's talk about God, the distinctive factor is that all the symbols are drawn from human life. God is never likened to any inanimate object; even when the reference is to the power of God, this is not expressed in terms of natural forces, but in terms of human authority. The implications of this human symbolism are very considerable. For one thing, we are to realize that God is to be found and expressed among people, not mainly among things. This seems to me to raise big questions about every suggestion that God should be conceived of in substantial terms. Not only are the substantial terms of orthodox statements like the Chalcedonian Formula out of date as notions of substance; any substantial terminology is inappropriate to express the nature of God, and the relations within the Godhead.

Another implication of the New Testament symbols applied to God is that the sphere in which God has most fully revealed himself is human nature. Therefore it follows that knowledge about human nature should be a fruitful source of knowledge about God. This is the area in which a new natural theology is being developed. As we know more about the meaning of human selfhood, we may learn something about divine selfhood. A deeper appreciation of the possibilities of human relationships should bring us to a deeper awareness of the possibilities of our relationship with God. This revelation of God in the human life of Jesus of Nazareth, with its startling insights into human relations, is not the final coping stone of the building which is knowledge about man. Rather, the revelation of God is found within the human relations. To live in reconciled relation with our fellows is to live in reconciled relations with

God; without the human reconciliation the divine relationship is void and valueless. It is surely the plain implication
of the gospel message, repeatedly emphasized in the Epistles,
that knowledge of God goes hand in hand with knowledge of
man, and also that relations with God are inextricably bound up
with relations with other human beings.

So modern theology has become Christocentric in its view of
God. This of course raises great problems, because at the same
time that we are centring our view of God upon the teaching
of Jesus, we are subject to a very great deal of doubt about the
authenticity of that teaching. We certainly appreciate that the
terminology which Jesus used, even that which looked simple,
like father, and judge, and king, nevertheless needs a great
deal of demythologizing. Yet as we have seen, this process does
not involve the idea that the terms mean nothing at all. They
must have some meaning if Jesus really is the revelation of God.
Do we really accept what he said, supposing that we can know
what it was? It is true that we question some things—his belief
in the authorship of the book of Moses, for instance, his dependence upon the details of the Law, his belief in angels and
the terminology about the coming end of the world. But at the
same time we seem to assume that other things that Jesus said,
that is, 'spiritual truths', are unquestionable. There is clearly a
great need for much further study of this question. This is particularly so because in the present situation many theologians
have a great enthusiasm for the idea of finding Christ in the
world; in our neighbour, and so on. But they seem often to
have lost sight of the possibility of finding Christ in Jesus. What
I mean by this is that we must take seriously what we mean by
the revelation of God in Jesus and we must be prepared to find
in this not a contradiction of natural theology, and not even the
final coping stone of the edifice without which the whole
building is useless. Rather, what we have to find in the revelation of God in Jesus is the clarification and usability of the concept of God. And this we shall do much more effectively if we
are aware of what in fact Jesus in his life has taught us about
God.

When we consider this matter more fully we find that it is not
only a case of considering the teaching of Jesus. Jesus reveals
God not only by speaking about him but by being divine.

There is, of course, the traditional reluctance to say Jesus is God. But equally there is in the New Testament the emphasis on the idea that in him dwells the fulness of the Godhead bodily. Jesus himself is reported to have said 'He who has seen me has seen the Father'; and 'I and the Father are one'. Both these expressions must surely be an indication of the conviction which was carried over to the Christian faith that there was about Jesus something more than the authenticity of his teaching. It was his life which expressed the nature of God. In his life we shall be able to see what God really is like. Here again modern theologians are providing very valuable insight into Christian understanding. For instance, William Hamilton makes a great deal of the idea that throughout his life Jesus was expressing humiliation, suffering and failure. We have long been accustomed to thinking of this as the full expression of the true nature of man. But we have been slow to appreciate that it is part of a full expression of the nature of God. It is God who is humiliated, God who suffers, it is God who knows what failure really is. This is the nature of God and we must not mar or blur this picture of God by quite natural ideas about the eventual victory of God. The victory of God is in the humiliation and the suffering and the failure, not in any eventual reversal of fortune.

This is how we can best interpret the resurrection. The resurrection is the expression of the power of God vindicating the revelation of the nature of God in the life of Jesus. It is no doubt also an expression of the power of God in Christ to overcome sin and death. But it must not be regarded as a final reversal of the revealing of God which has taken place through the life and death of Jesus. Rather, the resurrection seems to be the divine confirmation of the validity of the revelation of the nature of God which was made clear in the person of Jesus Christ. The resurrection is not in the normal sense of the word the happy ending which finally confirms the truth which otherwise would seem to be totally obscured. The resurrection is one of the ways in which the truth of God is made known in Christ, and we must not think of that truth as only revealed in supernatural and completely mysterious ways.

So God and man are revealed together. When we begin to understand this we can more fully appreciate that it is in the whole life of Jesus and in the continuing life of Christ in the world that God is revealed. This is not to be understood as a separation between God and man. David Jenkins in *The Glory of Man* has a very interesting way of expressing this point. 'When the love of God and the love of man really get down to it, they come to the same thing.'[1] This surely means that the nature of God is bound up with the nature of man. We cannot find God apart from man and we cannot know man apart from God.

One of the problems raised by this approach is the grounds on which these assertions can be made. The Christian answer here must surely be that this attitude to Christ rests on faith. This of course doesn't mean a contradiction of thought or a denial of reason. But it does mean that it is only possible through the eyes of faith to see the truth of God in Christ. The relation between faith and our knowledge of God is clearly very close. As Gerhard Ebeling says, 'Jesus is the essence of faith and faith is the essence of the work of Jesus.'[2] This is not only a way of saying that in the end a knowledge of God is not revealed to an unbelieving attitude. It is also saying two very important things. Firstly, this emphasis on faith means that God can only be known in a personal way as we know persons. There are great difficulties in talk about encounter with God, speaking with God, and so on. But there is no doubt that, to a Christian, to believe in God is to meet him in Christ; that is, in an encounter which can only be expressed as personal. This is an encounter in which the whole of our personal life is involved and we must put into it will, expectation, desire, and emotion. Only then can we really be said to be exercising faith. The other implication of this emphasis upon faith is that all talk about God which stops short of commitment is illusory. It is no use implying that we want to settle the question of whether God is or not before we will further decide whether we intend to do anything about it. There is no possible way of knowledge of God in this direction. To have faith in God means not only to believe that God is; it means at the same time, and inevitably involved in the same attitude, an attitude of commitment and obedience to God. Belief which has no existential responsibility, as some people would put it, is not Christian faith. So that the

[1] *Op. Cit.*, S.C.M. Press, p. 103.
[2] *Word and Faith*, p. 204.

centrality of Christ in the question of faith in God is not only that the meaning of faith and the possibility of language being used about God is clarified, but also we see the intimate relation between our attitude to God and the manner of life we intend to lead.

This leads me to a further comment about the relationship between Humanism and Christianity. One of the most damaging comments that the Humanist makes about the Christian faith is that it doesn't really matter whether we believe in God or not. We may well say that this is based upon a misunderstanding, and that we wish to correct it and to explain how vital belief in God is to a Christian. But we cannot avoid the conclusion that to some extent the Humanist has drawn this conclusion about the irrelevance of faith in God because of what he has seen of the Christian life. In the past, and also in the present, the Church has failed to some extent because it has over-intellectualized the concept of God. God is someone to be argued about, someone to be expressed in complicated and difficult phraseology. All this is a very poor substitute for the belief in God which is expressed in a manner of life. If Christians really were totally committed in their belief in God no one would have any possibility of arguing that belief in God is irrelevant. But too often it seems that our talk about God is mere empty sound without any meaning; the real tragedy is that so often our belief in God is not in fact practised in life. We have in this sense failed to learn the lesson which is absolutely central in the revelation of God in Christ. That is, that it is through the manner of life—not just through words but through a *life*—that belief in God is understood and expressed.

Parallel to this danger of over-intellectualizing God is the danger of over-humanizing him. It is obvious that one way of interpreting the contemporary theological emphasis upon the revelation of God in Christ is to argue that ultimately God and man are the same. This, I think, is very far from what is really meant in modern theology by the humanity of God. What Barth and others mean by this phrase is that God has committed himself to man permanently in Jesus. If we are to find God and meet him, we shall find and meet him in man; not apart from man. This doesn't mean that God and man are the same; but that God has permanently involved himself with humanity and will always be found among men. The implications of this are tremendous. For one thing, it means that all attempts to find God apart from humanity must be doomed to failure. Whatever value there is in a life of a hermit we must recognize that the basic Christian view is that we do not find God by running away from man, but by being involved with human life in all its mystery and in all its problems. Only when we are really involved with our neighbour shall we find God. This brings us back again to this question of our encounter with God in the central situations of life rather than in the occasional, external, temporary situations. As the significance of our life is in our involvement with people, so we shall find God in this involvement. This therefore means that far from the Incarnation meaning that God is dead, it is only in the Incarnation that we really see the life of God. Only in Christ can we hope to find the answer to the question of what we can say about God in our time.

We now come to the question of how all this can be applied in the schools situation. There is no doubt that the questions which have been raised occasion very serious problems as far as teaching religion is concerned. We need to remember that the old conceptions of God as a father figure, or as a super-human person, however outdated they may be, did seem to be reasonably understandable to children. But there is no doubt that this early intelligibility does give rise to later questions, because as children grow up they see more and more how impossible it is to hold on to these over-personalized conceptions of God. So let us not be too discouraged if we find the task of presenting God in new ways very much more difficult than formerly. It may be that at least we can hope to bring up children to a concept of God which they will not later have to abandon, as has often happened in the past.

There is great need to clear away many misconceptions which will be in children's minds about what we mean by God. It is still necessary to disabuse children of the idea that God is an old man in the sky, or a big brother who is continually watching us and especially watching every mistake we make. And equally, perhaps at a more sophisticated level, we need to be aware of the problem of the childish trust in God which assumes God does everything, implying that we have no need to

8

try to understand the world. This is no doubt in some ways a very laudable attitude, but it is not an attitude to be encouraged uncritically. If children are brought up with this idea, not only will it discourage them from doing the best they can to understand the world and their place in it, but it will also very easily give rise to the false notion that when things go wrong God can be blamed, because after all he does everything, so when things go wrong he's caused that, too.

In this connection there seems to me to be great value in stressing that faith in God is not just an intellectual assent, nor is it a violation of reason. The relationship between faith and love needs greater emphasis. It is probably true that few come to faith by intellectual approaches. It is rather the appeal of the warm humanity of Jesus which will often be the beginning of faith. The question whether it is suitable to attempt to arouse faith in God in children in schools needs a lot of consideration. Is this the job of the R.E. teacher, or is it best left to the Churches? If we answer 'the Churches', we have to face the fact that a great number of children with whom we have to deal will never have, apart from our influence, much chance of understanding what faith in God really means. We have to recognize that faith in God is only awakened by conscious effort, and if this is left out of the concept of teaching R.E., I fail to see how R.E. can ever be any more than a dry and irrelevant subject. Only if R.E. enables children to see Christianity as a way of life can it be a worthwhile subject.

Not only should we emphasize the relationship between faith and love in the concept of God, but we must also emphasize it in connection with the practical implications of faith in God. It surely is the business of R.E. not only to teach children sensible and sound ideas about God but to give them an opportunity of expressing this faith in God which develops as a result of our teaching. I would here very strongly commend the various activities which go on in many schools in connection with community service and various forms of help for people in need. This is, I think, the right way to express what we mean by faith in God. You will notice that immediately this brings into focus again the question of relationship with people. I do not think it is any use talking about faith in God separately from our responsibility to our fellow men. It is a very great drawback to

R.E. teaching if it is all theory and there is never any practice of it. There is a great need for R.E. teaching to take account of the way in which much of learning is emphasized and made secure through personal activity and personal inquiry. And wider experience of people can lead to a deeper experience of God.

This also relates R.E. teaching to the whole activity of the school. We are not concerned to add the icing to the cake, as one writer has put it—the solid matter of the cake being mathematics and English and languages and science and all the rest. Knowledge of God is found in all these things and is practised in their discovery and application. The integrating activity of the R.E. teacher must be a very considerable part of his responsibility. Rather than attempting to give additional knowledge of a different basis and with different means of verification from other knowledge, he is surely better employed bringing into focus the insights that the children gain from all their other subjects, demonstrating their significance in the light of belief in God and the expression of this belief in terms of responsibility to our fellow men.

7 | *What is wrong with us and How can it be put right?*

ONE urgent need of our time is to state the Christian message in contemporary terms. No longer are we able to speak to modern man about sin with the hope that he will understand our meaning. And yet the question 'What is wrong with us?' is still relevant to modern needs. Recently, in *The Observer*, Arthur Koestler discussed this very question. His argument was that the old traditional statements about the wrongs which arise from personal human attitudes of selfishness and so on are really wide of the mark. It is not only the failings of human character but perhaps even more the so-called virtues of courage and devotion and willingness to be a part of the community and to live according to that community's views which constitute a great deal of the human problem and gives rise to human suffering. Koestler is wrong, in fact, in his interpretation of the traditional Christian view of man's predicament; for that view has always been that it is not only man's so-called vices but also his supposed excellencies which can be the cause of trouble in the human situation. Yet we can at least accept part of Koestler's argument. There is something wrong with us and this is partly what religion is about.

It is true that a superficial view of life, especially in the western world, easily persuades us that there isn't really very much wrong at all. Our standard of living is continually rising; our range of interests is continually widened; our prospects for the future are much brighter than ever they were. All this is true, but it does not obscure and cannot deny the fact that there is still much that is wrong with the human situation. In a sense this is the concern of politics for politics deal with the practical attempt to improve the human lot. If there were nothing wrong in the human situation, there would be no need for laws, or for any Parliament; everything would be in perfect order and have no need of any sort of development at all. So the Christian message is not all that strange to modern ears. And yet there is something very strange about it, because what the Christian gospel seems to be asserting is wrong many people nowadays do not regard as wrong at all. Particularly, the Christian message seems to have emphasized the seriousness of personal faults and crimes like theft and sexual deviations, swearing, lying and theft. But many people think these are only peripheral problems. They believe that what is wrong with the human situation is not really attributable to human attitudes but to a system, to government, to the economic arrangements and so on. This raises very serious questions about the context in which the Christian gospel is to be preached. We have to recognize that a gospel inevitably implies that there is something wrong with the human situation. But it may be that to some extent the emphasis in the past upon individual faults has been overstated. We now need to see that what is wrong with us is not only that we are personally responsible for certain wrong attitudes, but that the system under which we live is itself very inadequate and in need of change. It is not that we must find at all costs a view of sin which will be popular, for surely no realistic view of sin can be popular. But what we must find is a view of the human situation which is at least relevant and intelligible. How do the modern theologians face up to this challenge?

Modern theologians have not yet said very much about the doctrine of sin. Indeed, it sometimes seems as if they have taken away from us not only our concept of God but also our concept of sin, and the latter may be as serious a deprivation as the former. Yet there are indications among some modern theologians of concern about this subject. For instance, Paul Tillich is very helpful in his discussion of the Fall. This is a reality in the human situation. It is something for which man must take certain responsibility; and sin is indeed a serious factor in the human situation. Tillich uses such terms as 'frustration' and 'estrangement' and, indeed, 'guilt', to describe what are the characteristics of the human problem. We have here some attempt to re-interpret the meaning of sin in a modern way that man can understand and which will encourage him to turn away from sin to a better attitude towards God and his fellow man.

Generally speaking sin is, of course, a theological expression. It can well be argued that, apart from belief in God, sin has no meaning. We can talk about faults, about crimes or mistakes, but unless we believe in God it does not seem possible to talk about sin. In contemporary popular Christian thinking sin has become pluralized. That is, we talk about 'sins' instead of 'sin'. From this develops the idea that there is a list of sins which we should try to avoid. This list often seems to be made up of attitudes which are not of the most serious significance. Some critics of the Christian faith point out that we Christians seem very good at castigating our contemporaries for such faults as gambling, drunkenness, sexual immorality, thieving, and so on. We are not so good, they say, at pointing out that the real problems facing mankind are poverty, racial discord, bitterness, economic hardness, insecurity, and the many problems which arise out of war. It does sometimes seem as if the Church is really only interested in talking about sins in a sense for which she seems to have an answer and in which her members are not much involved.

There is a further problem about the modern attitude to sin in the traditional evangelical view that normally a man should feel guilty in the sight of God for the wrongs, that is the sins, he has committed. Then he must be willing to recognize his faults in these matters. He must turn to Christ and ask for forgiveness, which is then given to him, and he is saved. There are several difficulties about this scheme. One is that, try as he will, modern man is often not able to feel guilty. He may feel frustrated, lost, embittered, lonely and many other things, but guilty he often does not feel—certainly not at the beginning of his religious pilgrimage. Another serious result of this traditional pattern of guilt and forgiveness is that man is encouraged to think that sin is something that is dealt with at the beginning of the Christian life and thereafter can well be forgotten.

Indeed, in some contexts it seems as if 'sin' is a word not to be used in polite Christian conversation. It may be applied to 'the others', that is, people who have not yet gone through this process of recognizing their guilt, asking forgiveness and becoming one of the converted. So that if one could have some way of registering the reactions of a congregation to the word 'sin' or 'sinners', I strongly suspect that one would find the immediate response in many people's minds to be 'that means other people, it doesn't mean us'. This, of course, is a very serious situation if it is anywhere near the truth, for it is precisely the problem of sin in believers, sin in the Church, which needs to be tackled.

Modern theology has not removed the concept of sin from religious thought. Rather it has placed it in a different situation in the religious life, not at its beginning but in course of the development of the Christian life. It is surely true that the closer man comes to God and the more he realizes his religious responsibilities, the more aware he is of his sin. There is great need for Christian people to recognize that there are faults in them which continually need correction, and for which they must seek the forgiveness of God. And this is also true of the Christian community, which needs continually to recognize in humility that it makes mistakes and is not infallible.

In arguing that we need a concept of sin which is at least understandable to our contemporaries, we are not saying that this view of sin will necessarily be acceptable or popular. Indeed, we can go further and say that there are certain aspects of the modern attitude to what is wrong with the human situation which should cause considerable disquiet. For instance, if the contemporary answer to the question, 'What is wrong with us?' is 'the system, the economic situation, industrialization etc.,' we are in great danger of removing far from our own area of responsibility every possibility of action. This means that we become less and less concerned about improving the situation and more and more ready to blame other people. One of the characteristics of modern man's attitude whenever he is in any sort of difficulty is that he looks around for someone to blame. The Government, the Church, even the weather can be blamed in their turn; but this is a false response to a difficult situation, because there is often a need to blame ourselves or to take responsibility for our own situation. Indeed, if we think that it is more comfortable and acceptable to be able to blame other people instead of taking responsibility ourselves, we do well to remember that a man without responsibility is to that degree less human than a man who accepts his responsibility and is prepared to take the blame.

This subject is often extremely difficult to teach to children. But there are certain aspects of it in which the approach of adolescents may be a help to us. Firstly, it is undoubtedly true that some adolescents do have a lively sense of guilt. It may be that in some cases the sense of guilt is wrongly aroused by situations which ought not to occasion it at all. It is also true that guilt is sometimes, perhaps often, an unhealthy attitude which certainly should not be artificially created. But it is still true that young people do know when they have done something for which they are responsible, and which is wrong, and they do know what it is to feel guilty about it. Since this is one of the very strong feelings that many adolescents do have, we are mistaken if we think this is not to be used in our presentation of the Christian faith to them. Secondly, the other situation which arises here is that young people often have a very vivid sense of the wrongs that are present in the world, often putting grown-ups to shame. For instance, children vividly sense the suffering of animals—and how strongly they react to information about famine, and so on. They feel very deeply that something ought to be done about it, and this is a reaction which has great positive possibilities. So that while we shall go on to argue that there is a lot that needs to be said about community faults as well as personal faults, it would be wrong to imply that there is nothing any more to be said to pupils about personal responsibility. One of the important features of a truly integrated life is the recognition of one's own responsibility and willingness to accept responsibility for one's own actions and to try to mend one's ways. To grow up is to grow in awareness of personal responsibility.

It seems, then, that there are two particular issues with which we have to deal in this connection. Firstly, there is the relationship between personal and corporate responsibility and problems. We cannot avoid the traditional conclusion that religion is partly about personal responsibility and personal faults. This is unavoidable. It is a necessary corollary of one of the precious truths of the Christian faith; that we are indeed each one of us persons in God's sight. This means not only that we have our personal responsibility to bear but also we have the assurance of a personal care of God over us. Those who argue against personal responsibility, as some behaviourist psychologists do, and those who claim that the environment is often the main factor in the formation of character, hardly seem to realize what they are doing. They are taking away from the human person his most precious feature, namely his responsibility as a person before God. Therefore it would be quite wrong for a Christian exposition of the problem of sin to avoid every reference to personal responsibility and personal fault. And yet at the same time there is the question of the corporate aspect of our faults. It must surely be quite clear to any thinking person that it is not enough just to say that each individual person has gone wrong and must himself somehow put his situation right. Again and again we face the fact that it is the system under which we live, it is our heritage, it is economic circumstances which all contribute very much to the sort of people we are. This cannot be denied. And it is the system under which we live which gives rise to so much human misery. Sometimes it seems as if all the Christian Church is saying is that if we were all better individuals the world would be a better place. This is hardly likely to be regarded as a revolutionary statement. Nor is it to be thought of as sufficient reason for a man to live as Jesus did and die as he did on a cross. It is far too obvious for any such interpretation. The modern generation is not content—and ought not to be content—to think only in terms of personal weaknesses, temptations, and so on. The big faults cannot be ignored. Unless the Christian faith has something to say about the large questions of poverty, war, and racial disharmony, then it really will be shown up as totally inadequate in our present situation.

The second problem that arises in this modern discussion of sin is this; granted that we have to think not only of personal but also of corporate faults, not only of the individual but also of the system, still it is not by any means apparent what religion has to do with the answer. Referring again to the contemporary question 'What is wrong with us?', it is noticeable that very rarely nowadays is religion thought to hold any solution to this problem. In the article I mentioned at the beginning of the chapter, Arthur Koestler does not see religion as in any way an answer to the problem. Indeed, it often looks as if modern man has dismissed not only the traditional formulation of religion, but also many worthy attempts to express it in practical terms. For instance, how easily our contemporaries despise the person they call 'the do-gooder'. It is interesting to ask why this should be so. Is it because modern man has an uneasy feeling that at least some people are trying to do something about the human situation, and their activities are in a sense a condemnation of his own indifference? Or is it because it is thought that these individual activities make so small an impression upon the total situation that they are not really worth considering? Whatever may be the reason for this peculiar attitude, we have to admit that, generally speaking, the majority of people do not think that religion has much to contribute to the solution of human problems as we now see them. Indeed, this is really only another way of saying that religion has largely lost its significance for many people. For if they thought it had any answer to the human problem, they would, of course, be far more interested in it. It is salutary to remember that, for most people, interest in religion is in direct proportion to what they consider to be the extent of its usefulness. If it is no longer thought to be useful or applicable, then the interest in it very quickly diminishes. For it is surely unquestionable that most men are not very deeply interested in the metaphysical questions which religion may raise. They are only interested in the manner of life and the solution to real problems that religion may produce. And if religion does not seem to be producing any of these solutions, then the interest in religion declines almost to vanishing point.

When we consider the possible Christian answers to the human predicament, we need to notice that it is now no longer sufficient for the Christian gospel to be concerned only with the personal situation. Whatever view of the Cross we may be able eventually to advance it must be concerned not only with how individuals are set right, but also how the whole human situation is affected by the events of the life and death of Jesus. This is a reminder that some of the views of the mean-

ing of the Cross which we may have to abandon nevertheless
have this advantage, that they speak of the cosmic or world-
wide significance of the life and death of Jesus, and this is something that cannot completely be forgotten. So in our consideration of the meaning of the Cross we must look for some way
of explaining what was done, not only in terms of personal
responsibility, but also in terms of the total human situation
which includes the threat and reality of starvation for millions,
violence and hatred becoming an accepted way of life, and the
deep divisions among different races. This is the world situation as it now is. The last thing we ought to be expecting from
religion is a harmony which is not found in the world at
large.

Religion is not a way of contracting out of the world. The
traditional views of salvation are also now often seen to be an
almost total failure because they offend against the deepest
convictions of man's moral sense. If we have advanced in any
way in our modern situation, perhaps it is in this, that there are
certain things, perhaps not very many, but certain things, of
which we are more than ever sure. One of these convictions is
that it is wrong for the innocent to suffer instead of the guilty,
and it is particularly wrong for punishment to be transferred.
We also recognize that punishment which is mainly vindictive
must be regarded as very inadequate, and possibly immoral. In
other words, we begin our consideration of the human predicament and the supposed religious answer to it with certain
convictions about what things are right and what things are
wrong. This is surely a very healthy way for a man to begin to
consider the meaning of the doctrine of salvation. Whatever
that doctrine is, it must not offend against the deeply held convictions which we have attained in our understanding of life
generally.

Some of the more theological problems arising out of the
traditional views of the Atonement are to do with the Protestant
doctrine of justification by faith alone. This is the view that, in
the predicament in which man is placed, he cannot in any way
save himself. Indeed, any attempt to save himself is only an
attempt at self-justification and can only end in further disaster.
Only by reliance by faith on the merits of Christ can a man be
reconciled to God. There is no doubt much significance and

truth enshrined in this traditional doctrine of justification by faith alone. But it must be admitted that it does also give rise to very real problems. For instance, it inevitably produces the passive attitude of the acceptance of a change of status which is effected by God alone and in which man has no part. It is often said of modern congregations and modern religious attitudes that they are too passive. But for generations Christians, certainly those in the evangelical tradition, have been taught that there is nothing they can do about their salvation, no effort they can make which will bring about any change in their status before God. All they can do is to rely upon what God has done. When it is realized and recognized that all this has been said for generations, it is not surprising that modern Christians are so passive. After all, they have been told again and again, times without number, that there is nothing they can do to effect their salvation, so they naturally conclude they ought not to do anything. They become entirely passive. Admittedly this is a wrong interpretation of the doctrine of 'sola fide', which ought never to be thought of as meaning that we have no responsibility and do not have to work out our own salvation. But it is undoubtedly true that this has been the effect of these traditional views of the Protestant doctrine of salvation.

Again, this emphasis upon the changed status has led to too much concern about the inner life of man. No doubt we do need to be concerned about the state of our soul and our relationship to God, but if this is our only, or even our primary concern, then we soon become self-centred, and of little use to mankind as a whole. Some people seem to find religion not a springboard for overt action but an alternative to action, and this is another unfortunate consequence of the traditional view of salvation. Against all this modern man realizes that what he needs and what the world needs is that he and the world should be better. Being saved means being a better man. If the world is saved the world will be a better place to live in, more peaceful, more orderly, more fulfilling, more satisfying for man. The question which the Christian doctrine of salvation has to face is, how can this be brought about? In the past it may very well have been that men were rightly concerned about their status, about their own inner situation, about their guilt before God and so on. But now surely the situation is that we can see much more clearly that the question we need to deal with is how we and the world can be made better than we are.

A further difficulty about the traditional views of Atonement, especially in the form of a satisfaction or substitution theory, is that they wrongly understand the teaching of the Bible. By this I mean that it is supposed that this satisfaction-substitution doctrine is the main teaching of the Bible about the meaning of the Cross. This is why this view is regarded as the orthodox view which cannot be changed—because it is taught in the Bible. And in so far as this view has a great deal of influence upon the hymns we sing and the interpretation of the meaning of the Cross to which we have been accustomed, it is not surprising that any attack upon this satisfaction-substitution view seems to be an attack upon the whole concept of salvation in Christ. But in fact this is a basic misunderstanding of biblical teaching. There is no single coherent doctrine or interpretation of the meaning of the Cross in the New Testament. What we have in the New Testament are many different ways of looking at the meaning and the method of salvation. It is as if we are pilgrims looking at a great cathedral. This marvellous building cannot be comprehended from any one viewpoint. From one angle one sees one aspect of it, from another angle another aspect. From a distance it creates one impression, from inside it creates another. If one takes the whole thing in one look, one gets a sense of its massive solidity. If, on the other hand, one looks carefully at the details of the carvings and stained glass windows, one has a view of another kind. All these views add up to something like a total concept of the significance, the beauty, and the meaning of the cathedral. But there is no one viewpoint from which the whole thing can be comprehended in one look.

The same is true of the Cross, except that the significance of the Cross makes even the most wonderful cathedral pale into insignificance. The men of the New Testament were so overwhelmed with the reality of the life and death of Jesus that they found it quite impossible to express its full meaning under any one theory or through any one illustration. So, according to their own situation, according to their own pre-suppositions and ways of looking at life, they expressed the meaning of the Cross in different ways. For example, the Cross is a means of ransom. Now this is an illustration taken from a system of slavery with which many people in New Testament times were all too familiar. A ransom is a means of payment of money whereby a slave can be bought from his owner and, if the new owner so wishes, he can be set free. Ransom, therefore, means paying a price. Ransom refers to the cost of our salvation.

On the other hand, every reference to sacrifice in the New Testament is obliquely or directly a reference to the ritual sacrifices of the covenant people of the Old Testament, especially to the sacrifices which took place in the sacred temple. Not only the word sacrifice, but every reference to the blood of Christ in the New Testament, is probably a reference to the sacrificial system. So the life and death of Christ can be regarded as a sacrifice. But in order to understand this we have to recognize the significance of the sacrificial background. We have to try to enter into the view of the relation between man and God, which is the assumption of the sacrificial ritual of the Old Testament. That is, that God has made it possible for man to approach him through these sacrifices. The offering of an animal, corn, or wine, or some other gift God has laid down, is the way through which his presence can be approached. It is perhaps a good thing for us to realize that if we could be transported into the situation in which the people of the Old Testament offered their sacrifices we should be appalled and probably disgusted. We should wonder how people could ever imagine that slaying an ox, and pouring part of its blood upon the altar and sprinkling part of it upon the people, had anything at all to do with the relationship between man and God. Yet we have to admit that there was a long period during which this was thought to be the way that God had appointed. It was not necessarily understood, although there was a theory about how it was supposed to work. The point of the references to sacrifice in the New Testament is not that it is supposed that instead of the sacrificial animal, Jesus himself is made the sacrifice, although sometimes in evangelical enthusiasm it has sounded as if the blood of Jesus is effective in more or less the same way as the blood of the sacrificial animal was effective. References to the sacrifice of Jesus indicate that through his life and death God has opened a new way to himself.

We need to notice, in considering the two most fundamental views of the meaning of the Cross in the New Testament, namely ransom and sacrifice, that these are quite separate views. They have really nothing to do with each other. Whatever ransom means, and however it could be effected, it was never thought that it could be effected through sacrifice. The only way to ransom a slave was through paying money. Equally, it was never thought that by offering sacrifices, anything could be done to ransom a slave. Indeed, the whole idea of slavery was abhorrent to the Jewish people among whom the sacrificial system developed. So we must recognize that here we have two ideas which cannot be put together into one theory of the meaning of the Cross and made into one coherent system. We can say the same thing with regard to the many references to justification. Justification is a legal word. It has to do with the way in which a guilty person can be regarded and treated as innocent by the judge. And the model of the relationship between man and God which is considered in justification is a law court. On the judgement seat sits God, who knows perfectly all that there is to know about the criminal in the dock, guilty man. The problem is that God in his righteousness and holiness must declare the criminal guilty and must condemn him to a proper punishment, which is death. The only way in which the predicament can be solved is by there being some intercessor between the guilty criminal and the righteous judge. The doctrine of justification, certainly in some of its later development, attempts to explain how Jesus Christ, who has no sins of his own for which he needs to be forgiven, can intercede on man's behalf before God, and how God can listen to this intercession and can treat man as innocent, that is, as justified, though he is guilty of sin which ought to bring him to death. Very many of the theories of salvation which have been used in Christian history have been over-dominated by this legal concept. It is surprising that Paul is so often claimed to be the instigator and the guarantor of the truth of this system, seeing that it was Paul himself who argued that Christ is the end of the law. This view of the Cross seems to put Christ in the straightjacket of the legal system. Again we notice that justification has nothing to do with sacrifice and it has nothing to do with ransom. We now have three views of the Cross, three points of view to consider.

But there are more. There is, for instance, the idea of

reconciliation which, indeed, is a view perhaps more attractive to us in our modern situation. This idea is that, by some means, the problem of the relationship between man and God is solved by Jesus becoming the agent of reconciliation. Somehow or other he has made peace with God. This is explained by Paul in some passages in terms of the union with Christ in his death and resurrection through baptism and faith. That is, Christ has become man for us; he has entered into our human situation; he has shared our life and death and he lives so that we can be truly united with him. The theory seems to be that the union between man and God is not possible without union in death; only with this can there be union in life also. It may be some help to say that this seems to be fairly close to the idea of what happens when a grafting of a tree takes place. A new plant cannot be grafted on to an old stock unless the old stock is cut and an incision is made. In the same way it is as if we cannot be grafted into Christ unless he has died and we are really united with him in death; then we can be united with him in life.

Another view of the meaning of the Cross which is also found in the New Testament is that Jesus has made a perfect offering of obedience. By this offering of obedience he has pleased God, and this offering, which is acceptable to God, has been made available to us through the eucharist. This is a view which is partly expounded in the letter to the Hebrews. Other views which are also used are propitiation and expiation. These are connected with the sacrificial system which I have already commented upon. Throughout the whole of the New Testament the clearest indication is that what Christ has done for us is something we could not do for ourselves; something of tremendous import and something that has indeed radically changed our whole situation.

One view which I have not yet mentioned, which I think is of considerable significance in view of what I said earlier about the community aspects of the meaning of the Cross, is that Jesus has achieved a great victory over the powers of evil by living and dying as he did. This view is particularly expounded in the Fourth Gospel. It seems to be of particular significance when we are asking the question 'Has the death of Jesus made any difference to everybody, to the whole situation in which men are placed?' This question can be answered, I think, if

we see that in Jesus there is the clash between the forces of good
and the forces of evil, and that Jesus himself has overcome the
powers of evil and has achieved victory for mankind. This
victory is available to man because Jesus himself was a man.

The conclusion we can draw from this view of the various
interpretations of the Cross in the New Testament is that as
people were situated in different contexts they interpreted the
Cross according to the view they had. The Cross did not mean
the same thing to everyone because everyone was not in the
same situation. This is surely an encouragement to us to look at
the Cross from our own situation. We must try to see its meaning from our own standpoint, not from somebody else's. This is
not to say that we necessarily dismiss all the interpretations of
the past as now false or valueless. Indeed, we can fully recognize
that many of these interpretations have served a very valuable
purpose in situations which inevitably are different from ours.
What we must not do is to suppose that our situation is the same
and that we can therefore only use the interpretations which
have been used in the past. We have to consider where we are,
we have to look at the Cross from where we are, to try to tell
our contemporaries what it means to us from where we stand.

So the question is, what does the Cross mean as we look at it
now? One emphasis of modern understanding of the gospels is
that we must begin with the life of Jesus. Whatever else modern
study of the New Testament has done, it has made much more
clear to us the significance of the life of Jesus. And there is a
great deal to be said for the emphasis upon that life as a life
lived for others. He was the man for others. In his whole life
we see an identification with the human race, an involvement
in human life which is the secret of our Lord's Incarnation. In
him there is full humanity. His life was lived always with a full
concern for those among whom he lived. It was especially
significant that his life was lived in very close involvement with
people who were poor, downcast, neglected, and despised. His
life was not just a life of meek acceptance, it was a life of protest
on behalf of the people among whom he lived. It was a life of
vision, of joy and hope, with a message which ordinary people
in their need could understand and to which they could respond.
This life was so much involved in the struggles and troubles of
ordinary people that inevitably he came into direct conflict

9

with the ruling classes of the time, especially the religious rulers. We need look for no other reason for the death of Jesus than that it was the natural and possibly inevitable culmination of a life fully involved with people. He lived for people and he died for people because he was not prepared to compromise his views of the demands of God for ordinary people. This brought him into such severe conflict with the religious rulers of his day that they found an excuse to put him to death. The death of Jesus was not an accident. Nor was it imposed upon an unwilling person by a vengeful God in order that satisfaction might be obtained for the sins of people. It was something that Jesus himself chose, which arose inevitably out of his life of sharing and caring for others. Jesus is therefore seen to be most fully one with us in this, that he not only lived a human life in all its limiting and frustrating conditions but he also died a human death. Which means that this person Jesus Christ, who cannot be fully comprehended in human terms, is indeed one who knows human life from the inside and fully shares it with us.

The first stage of this understanding of the meaning of the Cross is to realize the significance of this sharing of our life by Christ. Our life is fully shared by Christ in all its aspects. Of course there are limitations involved in Christ being a man, not a woman; in being a man who lived in the first century and not in the twentieth century. But a close knowledge of the life of Jesus, his teaching and his dealings with people will show us that everything that is significant in life he has shared and is able to understand. There is no situation in which man can ever be placed in which Christ has not himself shared. There is no situation of despair or sorrow or failure or frustration which we commonly experience, which Christ does not understand; and this understanding we are bound to say can only arise through an actual human life. The knowledge which we must assume God has of the human situation still would fall short of complete knowledge in that it would not be, apart from Christ, a knowledge of the human situation from the inside. But we can say that there is here someone who really shares human life with us.

The old adage 'a trouble shared is a trouble halved' is not any less true because it is old. This is something that in our own situation we find true again and again. We find often that its deepest truth is revealed to us in the context of Christian belief and Christian worship. For many people in the time of their bereavement, failure, or frustration, find within the fellowship of the Christian Church the way whereby their troubles are shared and halved. This is no contradiction of the point that I am making. For if among people troubles are shared and therefore halved, then it is reasonable to say that if Christ shares our trouble our trouble is halved. The first stage in understanding salvation is to realize the tremendous significance of this sharing of our life by Christ. This is not a total view of salvation but it is a first step on the way and one which is not to be despised. And I suggest that it is an attitude which many people can understand because, fortunately, most of us have known at some time or another how great a benefit it is to have someone to share our situation, and how much relief we gain thereby.

But this of course is still only the beginning of the understanding of salvation. If this were all we could say about Christ, then indeed we should not be saying anything which could merit the name of a gospel. So we have to move on to the second stage. Here I think we have to examine the situation in which Jesus was placed with regard to his opposition to evil. As I have already argued, one way of looking at the life of Jesus is to see it as a clash between the forces of good and the forces of evil, and to see it as Jesus' victory over evil. Now it is all too easy for us to assume that the only way to overcome is by force, by direct opposition, by conflict and by the exercise of great powers. This is not in fact the way that Jesus overcame evil. When we look at his life and death and resurrection we see that the powers of evil are overcome in him, not by retaliation and violence, but by acceptance and meekness. When he was reviled he did not revile in return. He met curses with blessings. He prayed for his enemies. He met every onslaught of evil by the absorbing power of love. Thus he conquered evil in a way to which evil had no reply. For we find in Christ the remarkable exhibition of the truth that if evil is met with true goodness, if goodness does not use the weapons of evil to fight it, if goodness accepts evils, in accepting it absorbs it. Then we see what real victory over evil is. For evil has no answer to this. If there could live a man so full of goodness and love and forgiveness that whatever evil did, he would never retaliate, never become bitter, never curse, and never seek to take revenge, then this man has conquered evil. And this is precisely what Jesus has done. He has overcome evil in the only way in which it can be overcome, by the all-absorbing power of love. Christ is so completely filled with goodness that he can—and does—take all evil into himself and absorb it; and thus he defeats it. It may be that this sounds too easy an answer to the problem of evil, and it certainly is true that there are some situations in which it is extremely difficult for us to apply it. Perhaps this is another way of saying that only such a person as Jesus Christ, who cannot be comprehended merely as human, but about whom one has to say that he is also more than human, only such a person could really live by this absorbing love in such a way as completely to defeat evil. But this is what Jesus has done, and this is his way of victory. Perhaps the resurrection is chiefly notable for this, that it is the outward expression of the victory which Jesus has already accomplished. It is not just the final happy ending to an otherwise unhappy story, but rather the expression of a victory which Jesus himself has won. So that there is in the message of the gospel the wonderful truth that by the way of love Jesus has conquered evil, and this victory is manifested in the fact that Christ is alive in the world and has conquered death and sin.

The consequence for us of the second stage of this view of the meaning of the Cross is surely tremendous. It means that not only have we in Christ the victor, the one who has conquered evil for us, but we also have in him the example of how we are to live and, in his strength, also to conquer evil. Both aspects need careful consideration. Firstly, we need to realize that this view of the Cross does mean Christ's actual victory over the forces of evil. This, incidentally, is what makes this view of the Cross different from the so-called liberal view of the past century, which could be summed up by saying that Jesus has shown the way to live and has given us an example which we must now go on and follow. True as this is, it is inadequate. The view that I am expounding is rather that we have in Christ the one who has for us overcome evil. 'The powers of hell have done their worst, but Christ their legions hath dispersed.' Such a note of victory in the Christian view of the Cross needs continual emphasis.

This victory is the basis of faith. To believe in Christ is to believe that his victory over evil is total and effective. The other aspect to consider is that we do have here a way of living which is commended to us. The way to accept the victory of Christ over evil, the way to have faith in Christ, is to live according to this love and in the power of this love. One of the advantages of this view of the Cross, it seems to me, is that it does have practical application in our own situation. It means that in many different conditions men who believe in the salvation of Christ must be prepared to live in the way that Christ lived, in the power that is made available to them through faith in him. Let me try to illustrate this from one or two human situations.

Most people know at some time in their lives what it means to receive personal insults. These are sometimes partly justifiable, partly not. And the natural reaction is to retaliate, to hit back, to give as good as we have received. It doesn't take a lot of imagination to see that out of this sort of retaliation arise most of the human problems in the world today. The Christian way in such a situation is to receive the insult but not to pass it on; to refuse to be a link in the chain of reaction which passes on insult and increases it in the process of passing it on. Another illustration can be taken from the prevalent habit of gossip, which so often vitiates good human relationships. The Christian attitude to the evil which is in gossip when, for instance, unkind and harmful and hurtful things are said about other people, is to let the gossip stop with us. We do not need to pass it on. We can hear it and there it can stay. We have in that sense absorbed it and to that degree, small though it may be, we have conquered a little bit of evil. The same sort of thing can be applied to a situation of more serious harm which is sometimes done to us by other people. It is natural to retaliate, to seek revenge, to go to law, to take our revenge and to have our recompense. But however natural this may be we have to recognize that again and again it only leads to further bitterness and further conflict. If only we could learn the lesson that Christ teaches us on the Cross, we should find that the way to overcome evil is not to retaliate, but to accept it, to absorb it, and thus to conquer it. I am ready to admit that is not by any means an easy answer to larger problems of relationships between nations and communities. I think it leads us, if we take it seriously, very close to a pacifist position, although there are other factors which have to be taken into account when one is considering one's responsibility to nations and to one's community. But I certainly urge that the way to believe in Christ, the way to accept the power of his Cross, is to live in the way that he lived and thus to become better people. This is not a matter of trying to save ourselves; it is a matter of becoming better people, and this, as I have already said, is what I think salvation is about. It is not mainly about feeling better, or having a different status, or being able to explain what has happened in abstruse and complicated relationships. It is a matter of being better people; and the way of Christ is the way of love, the way of absorption which does lead to better people and to a better world.

Before we leave this exposition, it is necessary to say something about its relationship to former theories, especially to the moral influence theory and also to the question of the costly sacrifice which Christianity has traditionally spoken of in connection with the death of Jesus. Firstly, I would claim that this is not really the old moral influence theory which emphasized Jesus' example but left us to get on with the job of following it. The moral influence theory avoided any reference to the objective reality of Christ's work for us, but the view I am proposing argues that there is an objective work of Christ which has been done for us. That is to say, through the life, death and resurrection of Jesus, a change has taken place in the nature of things. This is the only basis on which we can ever hope to live the life of love in following the example of Christ. The view outlined also takes some insight from the sacrificial theory which speaks of Christ as our representative rather than as our substitute. But does it make salvation less costly? This is the objection that many people make to it, and especially to any suggestion that sacrificial language no longer has much significance in our time. My answer to this is that we cannot possibly over-estimate how costly this way of love was and still is. I would certainly be far from denying any part of the agony which Jesus suffered on the Cross, sharing human life as he did. This agony is not to be comprehended simply in terms of physical suffering, but involves an attitude of complete identi-

fication with man and full sensitivity to the human situation.
Indeed, the point I am making emphasizes rather than mini-
mizes the suffering of Jesus, for it relates it not only to the Cross
but to the whole of his life. And I am sure that a serious attempt
to follow out the implications of this view of the victory to be
gained by all absorbing love will soon show us that this is in
fact no easy way for us, any more than it was for Jesus. It is a
way which makes great demands upon the human spirit,
demands so great that they can only be met by full reliance on
the power of Christ to continue to do in us what he did first in
his life and death on the Cross. And the victory which is
signalized and symbolized by the resurrection is a victory which
does become ours as we live in this way of love ourselves.

It remains for us to consider how this view may be applied to
the situation which meets us in schools. Firstly, I would maintain that the concept of estrangement, frustration, failure,
doubt and sorrow is far more understandable to children than
the concept of sin, which has become mainly without meaning
to most of them. In any situation in which human beings are
involved there arises the possibility, maybe even the certainty,
of estrangement. Most children know from very early days what
it is to be frustrated and what it is to fail, and they come to
realize that these are real situations, not to be shrugged off as
something that they will grow out of, but rather part of
total human life. This understanding will, it seems to me, raise
real response among children. Further, the undoubted fact
that many children in very early days do feel frustrated and
know a sense of failure has to be much more related to the concept of faith than hitherto. The relationship is not easy, but
if we can at least make it plain that faith in God centred in
Jesus Christ is about the sort of situation we have to meet, not
about the situation which we are not meeting, then we shall
have made some progress in helping our pupils to understand
what is the meaning of the life and salvation of Christ.

Again, the view of the life of Jesus which I have outlined
refers to the fact that his life was a life of rebellion against
injustice, persecution and poverty on behalf of those who were
so often despised and ill-treated. This surely is an attitude which
raises considerable response in the idealism of youth. One of
the great needs of our time is to relate this idealism to faith. It

is much to be deplored that the idealism of youth is often dis-
counted and stamped upon by those in authority because it
leads sometimes to outbursts of protest and disorder. This is a
tragedy, because youthful idealism is a very precious com-
modity, and we do well to remember that at the centre of the
Christian faith is one who expresses idealism in revolt against
injustice, and one whom young people have always been very
much inclined to follow because they see in him the way to a
meaningful life.

I need hardly stress the fact that it is possible to apply in all
sorts of situations in a school the concept of Christ's condescen-
sion and care for others as a basis for an unselfish and caring
life. There are already many indications that young people do
respond to an appeal for concern for others, and in the life of
the school they can very well learn that true leadership is to be
exercised not in bullying, or in domination and in terrorizing,
but in unselfish service for other people, caring for those in
need, the physically handicapped, the poor, the aged, and so
on. I maintain there is very good reason for hope here, for again
and again young people surprise and humiliate us by their concern for those who are less well off than they are, and who are
in positions of difficulty and disillusion. The view of the Cross
of Jesus which I am advancing here must surely be an encouragement to that sort of life of service and a way of expressing in life an acceptance of Christ's salvation. We must
repudiate the idea that to accept the way of Christ is only to run
away from life's problems and to be goody-goody and pious.
Rather, it is a way of active participation in human affairs, for
this is after all how Christ lived. He was fully involved in human
life; he was no hermit, he was no recluse, but one who lived
human life to the full. This may lead us further in the direction
of understanding that religious experience is really life lived to
its full capacity, and that this involves not only finding all the
satisfaction we can in our own pursuits, but finding even
greater satisfaction in caring for others and living for others.

Lastly, I think this view of the meaning of the Cross does
depend to a very large extent upon the reality of the relationship between Christ and the believer, at whatever age the
believer may be. You will have noticed that several times
during this exposition I have said that this way of forgiving love

is only possible in the strength of Christ. This is a specially meaningful way of talking to those who are nurtured in the life and worship of the Christian faith. Worship in the school, then, must be closely related to the way of life which is being advanced. And the total life of the school must be under the influence of the worship. The impatience of many children with school assembly probably arises from the fact that they see no relation at all between what goes on in the worship and what goes on in the school for the rest of the day. If there is no connection, then surely the children are right to be dissatisfied about their worship. If, on the other hand, the worship is a gathering together of the total life of the school in its concern for those in need and in its total concern for the discovery and living out of a full human life through learning and adventure, then worship becomes meaningful to those who take part in it. This way of life in Christ is not possible unless it is nurtured in Christian worship. Christian worship is the worship of a community, which in the case that we are considering is the school; and worship expresses its convictions not only in its hymns and prayers, but in the way the whole life of the community is directed.

8 | *Christian Living in a New Style*

FOR many people the ethical implications of theology are more important than the theology itself. It is often noticeable that people are more concerned about the moral implications of radical new theology than they are about the theology itself. The truth involved in this misunderstanding is that certainly religion is not just something to argue about and to discuss. Religion is about a way of living, and unless it can be shown that the new theology is affecting the way of living of our generation it will have little chance of impressing itself upon thoughtful people of our time. It is noticeable that again and again the criticisms of traditional Christian morality arouse a great deal of antagonism. For instance, the Quaker report on sex caused many people to express violent opposition to any such change in accepted attitudes. Harvey Cox, discussing the moral implications of Christian faith in *The Secular City*, aroused a great deal of opposition when he expressed views contrary to normal and accepted standards of morality. Yet it would be a mistake to conclude that modern theologians are more interested in destroying the old moral framework than in providing an alternative. The question we must first deal with is what are the criticisms of the traditional attitude to morality which are being presented by modern theology?

Robert Adolfs, in *The Grave of God*, argues very strongly on this issue. He accepts the view of many of his contemporary theologians that religion is not to be regarded as something that is necessary to solve the problems of human life. It is noticeable that the norm he applies to religion and to morality is what is satisfactory for human living. He argues that too often in the past Christianity has been too much concerned with a supposed situation arising after death. On the contrary, he insists, Christianity is about a way of life which is applicable in the present or it is of no significance to us. He further criticizes traditional Christian views for being too exclusively applied to the private sector of life. Repeatedly the emphasis in Christian responsibility is only in terms of what the individual must do to live out his life in the given circumstances of modern civilization. This often leads to a half-hearted asceticism or a tendency to suspect the fulfilment which is available in many spheres for people in this modern world. Against this over-emphasis upon the private sector of life, Adolfs argues that the Christian style of life should be also applied to those powers and influences which are formative for human life. By these powers he means, for instance, ideologies, institutions and political systems. It is in these areas of life also that the Christian standard must be applied. From these areas of life must be discovered the full humanity which is the Christian aim, or else these forces must be opposed. This also leads to a criticism of some tendencies to secularization. When secularization develops into the secularist view which disregards every factor in life except that which can be weighed or measured or subjected to scientific tests, it is an imposition upon human life of an alien force which inhibits man's full humanity. One interesting exhibition of this approach is when some scientists urge us that it is necessary for them to press on with scientific inquiry at all costs, but steadfastly refuse to accept any social responsibility for the discoveries they make. This is, maybe unwittingly, inflicting upon man an external influence which is destructive of his full humanity.

Adolfs asserts that it is not enough for the Church merely to criticize modern man's inability to apply his faith to his ideology. The Church must itself abandon its own power-structure, which has been built up over the centuries, in order to be able to demonstrate the truth of its teaching that the Christian way can be, and indeed must be, applied to the public sector as well as the private sector of life. He argues that this involves for the Church a process of *kenosis*, or self-emptying, rather than *aggiornamento*, or adaptation. This is a reference to the assertions made in the preparatory discussions leading up to the Second Vatican Council which speak of the need for a renewal of the Church. But, says Adolfs, such a renewal implies a renewal of the power-structure of the Church. He asserts that the Church has to learn not a new *power*-structure but the place of poverty, humility and humble acceptance of the servant rôle. Only if the Church does this, will she be able to show that the Christian way of life which is being seriously applied to the structure of the Church can also be applied to the power-structure of the world. What is envisaged in all this is that in a real sense the kingdoms of this world must become the kingdoms of our Lord and of his Christ. In the past the Christian teaching often tended to ignore the kingdoms of this world and to imply that it was no business of the Church to think about changing these power-structures. This has led to a first-aid attitude rather than a radical cure. The Church has been there to pick up the casualties of modern life, but has not been at all concerned to re-fashion the roads and the vehicles so that the accidents will not happen.

Another interesting discussion of the new style of living is found in William Hamilton's *New Essence of Christianity*. One of Hamilton's valuable suggestions is that the new style of Christian living will reject the old, interfering type of Christian action. The traditional Christian attitude often seems to have been 'I've found the right way to live, now I will show you, teach you, if necessary force you into it'. It is this assumed superiority and arrogance which our contemporaries find especially distasteful about many Christians' attempts to apply their morality to the modern world. The world sees no reason to accept the arrogant claims of the Church to have discovered the right and only way to live, and is especially suspicious when the things the Church talks about are often not really dealing with the deepest problems that affect human life. In some ways contemporary secular morality seems to have higher standards than that sort of interfering Christian arrogance. For instance, modern man at any rate pays lip-service to the idea of privacy and tolerance. He does not think it is right to impose his own ideas upon other people, and he resents others trying to impose their ideas on him. There seems to be a fairly close relationship between this secular attitude and the attitude of Bonhoeffer which is expressed in one of his lesser known, but very important books, the volume on *Ethics*. In the course of the discussion in this work, Bonhoeffer says that the Christian has two responsibilities. To himself he has the responsibility of finding a full life and living it in Christ. For others he has the responsibility of helping them to have the means whereby they can decide freely for themselves how they can live the full life. Notice that Bonhoeffer does not say that it is the Christian's responsibility to tell other people what the full life is. They must be given the conditions of choice—freedom from poverty and political domination, and so on—and having been given these conditions they must be left to make up their own minds as to the way they want to live. This, of course, is a very far cry from the old traditional attitude of Christendom that the Church alone knows what is good for people and the Church must therefore not only tell people what to do but if necessary compel them to do it for their own good. A notable feature of this discussion is that we sometimes find more truly Christian morality being expressed outside normal and traditional Christianity than we find inside the Church. This is one of the interesting, and possibly disturbing, features of the modern situation. It may well be argued that the secular world has learned its moral principles from the Christian faith which it has now rejected. Nevertheless it is undeniable that in the outworking and application of these principles the secular world seems sometimes to have advanced beyond the rigid authoritarianism which is still typical of the Church in many of its attitudes to morality.

Bonhoeffer also raises an interesting question about the relation between the good life and the life of faith. He agrees that faith is necessary to produce the good life in its fulness, but he also argues that the good life in some sense is a precondition of faith. This means that there is some sense in talking about 'the Secular Saint'. That is, there is a way of life which is possibly preparatory to a fully Christian style of life, and this way of life can often be found among people who do not yet accept the full Christian faith. The fact that they have lived an ordered, reasonable, and responsible life is not a matter to be derided or ignored by the Christian. There is the danger that Christians can come to have a vested interest in the breakdown of secular morality. Indeed, some exponents of the Christian faith seem to delight in finding examples of the wickedness, stupidity, and total irresponsibility of their contemporaries. This is really based on the false assumption that unless a person accepts the particular form of the Christian faith which is being propounded, there is no hope of his living a good life. So when he seems to live a good life it is necessary to indicate that this can only be superficial, and is really very far from the good life as it ought to be lived. Surely this sort of carping criticism is no recommendation of the gospel being proclaimed by such exponents of the Christian faith. We must be ready to admit that there is a great deal of commonsense and responsibility and real concern evidenced by people who make no pretensions at all to Christian faith. It is far better to recognize this and honestly admit it—and indeed, to welcome it—than to assume that there is some skeleton in the cupboard if only we can find it.

The discussion so far has revealed one of the big questions raised by the new style of Christian living. That is, in what way, if any, is this Christian style of living different from the accepted humanist or secular style of living? It may be argued that there is no need to indicate a difference. Why should there be any difference at all? On the other hand, there are good grounds for saying that in the past one of the outstanding characteristics of the faith of the Christian was that it led to a different standard of life, a different quality of living, compared with that of his agnostic or unbelieving contemporaries. And it would certainly be very difficult to maintain the significance and value of Christian faith if its outcome were no different from a secular or humanist way of thinking. Therefore it does seem necessary for Christians to think more deeply about the characteristics of the Christian style of life in order to uncover the real principles which are involved in the application of the Christian faith. One possible way of looking at this is to say, as Hamilton does, that the Christian way of life is a peculiar blend of rebellion and resignation. We have to learn the way of resignation, that is, the acceptance of given conditions which cannot be altered; and we have to apply our faith to these conditions without grumbling and without resentment. On the other hand, the Christian is also called to make the world a better place. The application of the Christian gospel to life as it is must always be concerned with making life better. Clearly there is considerable difficulty in balancing these two paradoxical attitudes, but there is perhaps a good deal of truth in the argument that the Christian style of life is indeed a combination of rebellion and resignation. The words of Reinhold Niebuhr's prayer are worth remembering: 'O Lord, grant me serenity to accept things I cannot change, the courage to change the things I can and the wisdom to know the difference.'

But we shall have to dig deeper still if we are to find the real significance of the new style of Christian living. One necessary preliminary to such investigation is a study of the reasons for the contemporary situation. Is the Christian man necessarily committed to what is known as 'situation ethics'? That is, are there no longer any fixed rules which must be applied whatever the circumstances, but in each situation must the Christian decide for himself in the light of all the factors what his activity should be? The exponents of 'situation ethics' tell us that it is difficult, if not impossible, to make Christianity into a system of rules of conduct which can have universal application. On the other hand, those who oppose the attitude of 'situation ethics' seem continually fearful that the essential nature of Christian morality is being abandoned. They suspect that what is being expounded as Christian morality is really a weak acceptance of the contemporary views without any attempt to apply a Christian standard to those views. If we are to make some sort of worth-while judgement about this matter, we shall first need to look at how the situation which I have just been outlining has arisen. In other words, what has happened to the old rules which used to be identified with Christianity? How is it that in our time, perhaps as never before, this question of the possibility of different ways of applying the Christian faith can be spoken about?

The first matter which has to be noticed is that this questioning of the authority of Christian rules is part of a general questioning of authority, which is symptomatic of our time. The questions that our contemporaries ask are no longer merely an inquiry about what is the nature of the good life. Rather, the point that is being questioned is why should we even try to live what is called 'the good life'? This is particularly attractive to many of our young contemporaries because it does seem as if the rules of morality with which society has worked in the past are carefully designed to prevent human happiness. Or to put it another way, in the eyes of many young people, moral rules express middle-aged, middle-class morality, a way of security and respectability which is no longer acceptable to the young, nor to a wider range of society than those middle-class citizens who tend to think that their way is ideal.

Secondly, we have to notice that any system of morality based upon rules is always going out of date. The changes which take place in society inevitably mean that the rules of one generation fall into disuse in a succeeding generation for the simple reason that the social conditions make observance impossible or social standards make it no longer commendable. A good example of this is Sabbath Observance. The Victorian view of the matter was partly based upon an agrarian manner of life in which it was more or less possible for one day in seven to be set free from labour. But the increasing complexity of urban civilization makes this less and less possible. It is now realized that it is just not on for everyone to down tools on Saturday and not lift a finger to do any work until Monday morning. If this were done there would be no electricity, no public transport, no services of any kind, and we all know that this is neither possible nor desirable. The changing social conditions regarding Sunday Observance have created an atmosphere in which those who do not wish to attend worship see no reason at all why they should not do other things which in former days would have been frowned upon. And it is noticeable that increasingly even those who are closely connected with the life of the Christian Church do not apply the rigorous Victorian rules about Sunday labour that used to be universal.

Again, the old rigid rules applied by many Christians about total abstinence are now seen to be no longer of serious significance because the social problem with which these rules were meant to deal is no longer of the same serious proportions. So modern Christians find it very difficult to understand why there should be a rigid rule about taking alcohol, at any rate in moderation, when this does not seem to have much to do with living a Christian life. But I fancy that the greatest cause for the present disregard of the old-fashioned rules of Christian morality is the patent fact that many of these rules are just not relevant to the big issues which are facing mankind. The problems of poverty and race and war do not seem to be dealt with by these clear rules which for so long have been regarded as the essence of Christian morality. A morality which only deals with peripheral issues and steadfastly refuses to handle admittedly explosive but necessarily significant problems of human affairs cannot long retain the respect of thinking people.

The third reason why Christianity based upon rules has come under serious criticism is that the application of the rules often seems to cause greater harm than the breaking of them. For instance, take a somewhat hackneyed but nevertheless still possible illustration. The parents who reject and disown their erring daughter because she announces she is going to have a baby can now be seen to be acting in such a seriously defective way as to bring their own rule of mere respectability under serious condemnation. Many people would say that whatever wrong the girl has done is far outweighed by the wrong done to her by her parents if they reject her. If, in the time when she most needs understanding and love, they drive her out of their respectable lives and try to express by their action their abhorrence of the supposed breakdown of all morality, this can only lead to bitterness, frustration and despair. The application of the rule of respectability is worse than the breaking of it. Yet two wrongs don't make a right!

Again, we are slowly learning that many of the problems connected with homosexuality are not the responsibility of the individual. It may very well be that there are many cases in which the expression of homosexual tendencies harmful for society are culpable acts of responsible people. But we are coming more and more to recognize that some people are so made that the only expression of love that is possible for them is of a homosexual kind. At any rate, we are surely now aware of the fact that to put a homosexual in prison because his action is not in agreement with the commonly accepted, that is, hetero-sexual activities of the majority of the population, far from being just or helpful, will only drive him into further despair and frustration. Again, the application of the rule of morality, which is often no more than respectability as understood by the majority of the population, leads to far greater harm being done to human lives than the breaking of the rule. You will notice that the standard being adopted here is that which conduces to the greatest amount of human welfare and true fulfilment. I am not unaware of the difficulties which arise if utilitarianism becomes the only standard whereby the goodness of actions can be judged, but what I am arguing here is not a return to the old utilitarianism but rather that the standard of the truly good action must be whether it conduces to the full humanity of the society in which the action takes place. Most people still feel the need for rules, since a complete breakdown of morality would do no one any good. But the rules must be ruled by compassion.

The fourth and last reason I adduce for this contemporary widespread criticism of the old legal Christianity is that it was based upon an arrogant assumption that we Christians know best what is good for people, and we have a duty to impose our will upon others. Those in the Church often regarded themselves as guardians of morality and it is this assumption which is now seriously questioned. For one thing, as we have seen earlier in our discussion, our society is no longer ready or willing to be dominated by religious attitudes. This religious domination of society has been rejected in education, and in politics, and is now being rejected in morality. And I for one would not be willing to regard this as unfortunate. I think it is far better than this old stranglehold of authoritarian Christianity should be broken. The assumption underlying this traditional approach was that Christians have access to information about what is right and wrong which is not available to other people. Increasingly, those who claim to be Christians wonder just what this information is. We are often as much in the dark as anyone else as to what is the right and the wrong in any particular situation. We must agree with H. J. Blackham that Christians have no monopoly of 'high seriousness', as he calls it. We are not the only people who are thinking seriously about ethical problems; and further, Christians no longer have the confidence, or as I should put it, the audacity, to assert that we have all the answers and all people have to do is to be like us. This questioning of traditional moral codes is no doubt very disturbing to many people, especially of the older generation, but those of us who have to deal with the younger generation must recognize that in many ways the maintenance of the old position with regard to Christian rules is untenable. We must be careful not to waste our time trying to maintain a situation which is no longer defensible.

In view of these very serious criticisms of legal Christianity, it is not surprising that many modern thinkers, including new theologians, accept the inevitability of some sort of situation ethic to replace the old legal system. That is, there are no rules, everyone must please himself, and it is no longer possible for the Christian Church to attempt to teach the rules of life to the young or to anyone else. Before we jump to the conclusion that this is the only alternative to the old legalism, we ought to look a little more closely at the paradoxical situation which is presented to us in the New Testament. For the fact is that it can quite easily be shown that in the early Church both what we now call 'situation ethics' and what we now call 'legalism' were accepted as possible ways of Christian behaviour. Firstly, let us look at a good example of 'situation ethics' as outlined by St Paul in his letter to the Romans Chapter 14. The subject that Paul is dealing with is a good one for our purpose, for the subject itself is largely irrelevant to our modern situation, so we shall not be too emotionally involved. It was the problem of whether a Christian should eat meat which had been bought in the shambles, knowing that it had been sacrificed to idols. If he ate this meat, it could be argued that he was supporting the worship of pagan gods. If, on the other hand, he refused to eat the meat, was he not in danger of being overscrupulous and applying a new rule of morality which was an unnecessary addition to the Christian way of life? The problem hardly rises for modern man at all, but the principles upon which Paul discusses this issue are more clearly revealed because the subject matter is irrelevant to us.

Paul's attitude seems to be quite clearly in favour of a kind of 'situation ethic'. 'Who are you to pass judgement on someone else's servant?' he asks. 'Everyone should have reached conviction in his own mind.' 'Let us . . . cease judging one another, but rather make this simple judgement: that no obstacle or stumbling-block be placed in a brother's way. I am absolutely convinced, as a Christian, that nothing is impure in itself; only, if a man considers a particular thing impure, then to him it is impure' (NEB). In other words, Paul was very strongly against the reimposition of legal rules which were so typical of the Jewish attitude. He was not prepared to say that it was necessary for a Christian to abstain from eating meat sacrificed to idols, because this would be imposing a new condition on Christianity which denied its freedom and its dependence upon Christ. It seems as if, in this case at any rate, St Paul can be quoted in support of an attitude which refuses to add to the rules of Christian living, which are the basic rules of love and sympathy and toleration.

But on the other hand, if we look at the Sermon on the Mount, we find that there is a legal tradition in Christianity which cannot easily be denied. The illustrations we can adduce from the Sermon on the Mount, unlike those taken from Romans 14, are indeed very relevant to our contemporary situation. For instance, there are quite definite directions about the conditions of divorce. 'But I say to you that everyone who divorces his wife, except on the ground of unchastity, makes her an adulteress and whoever marries a divorced woman commits adultery.'[1] This statement is the basis upon which many Christians affirm that in no circumstances is divorce allowable to Christian people. The main tradition of the Church is pretty consistent upon this matter. Here is a definite command of the Lord which a Christian must be prepared to accept. It is admitted that often many cases of hardship will be caused, but it is argued on the other hand that if the rule is not kept, or if it is not made the standard whereby marriage is to be judged, the resultant hardship would be far greater than that which is caused by occasional, even quite frequent, breakdowns of marriage relationships. This is, of course, a matter of considerable difference of opinion between the denominations, and there are some who cannot see how this one rule can escape the principle which seems to be basic to our Lord's teaching, that forgiveness is the way in which mistakes and faults can be dealt with. If forgiveness is the royal road to dealing with errors, then some modern Christians find it very difficult to understand why of all the mistakes that a man or woman can make, mistakes made in connection with the marriage bond are

[1] Matthew 5:32 (RSV).

unforgivable. This view assumes that fully carried out, forgiveness includes restoration. But it is at any rate possible to see that there is here a considerable tension in Christian thinking which is by no means resolved at the present. The *avant garde* thinkers may be ready to say all sorts of forward-looking and sometimes even preposterous things about 'situation ethics', but the rule of the Churches remains more or less unalterable.

I am aware of the danger of trying to resolve a paradox by changing it into a compromise. Yet it is surely obvious that something other than the assertion of a paradox is needed in this particular situation. On the one hand, there are those who say that the whole Christian morality has collapsed, and no longer needs to be regarded at all. On the other hand there are those who maintain that the only possible course for Christians in our present situation is to maintain the legal view, the traditional standards of morality, because this is the only thing which is preventing modern society from disintegrating into complete chaos. Somewhere between these two extremes some sort of solution has to be found. I think it ought also to be recognized that in this dilemma facing the Church there is an even greater dilemma facing young people. It is especially difficult for the young to have to find their own way unaided in the extreme complexity of moral problems. Youth is by nature insecure, but it is made needlessly more insecure if the older generation is not able to hand on a reasonable standard of behaviour which will commend itself to the minds and emotions of the young. The older generation fails the younger generation if there is no reasonable standard which is recommended by its words and its life.

At the risk of being accused of taking more notice of Paul than of the Gospel according to St Matthew, I want to turn to the consideration of the passage in Romans, to which I have already referred. It does seem to me that we have in the discussion in Romans the thought of a Christian who is tackling a very difficult and practical problem which had arisen among the people for whom he felt responsible. If I were pressed I should have to say that I think that there is more consideration for the full meaning of the Christian faith in this passage than sometimes appears in the legalism of the Sermon on the Mount.

But let us not argue unduly about the comparative value of different sources. There are, it seems to me, certain principles adduced by Paul in this discussion which are worthy of our careful consideration.

Firstly, it is to be remembered that the whole discussion takes place in a corporate situation. This is not only with regard to the fact that this was a question which had arisen within a Christian community, although this is itself an important factor. But one of the principles which Paul is advancing is that every decision of this kind has to be taken within a societary context. The way Paul puts it is this: 'None of us lives to himself and none of us dies to himself.' This is surely the permanent condition of every moral judgement. One of the easiest pitfalls in this whole subject is to suppose we can make our decisions about what we do without any regard for other people or for the situation in which we are placed. Indeed, the very complications of moral decisions often conspire to persuade us we can only think about our own situation because this is difficult enough itself. We cannot possibly be expected to consider other people as well. But every moral code, every attempt at a moral attitude in society, is bound to take into account the fact that we are a part of a community. We do not live to ourselves, and this certainly is one of the contributions that the Christian view of morality is bound to make. It must make this contribution all the more because one of the tendencies of modern civilization is that through increasing economic prosperity we think that we are more independent. It is not without significance that it is still common to hear of a person of 'independent means'. This apparently refers to the idea that such a person is not dependent upon other people for a job or for maintenance or perhaps goodwill or support. Now it is true that some people do think that they are in such a position. Quite often the person who regards himself as 'self-made' is inclined to think that he has by his own efforts reached a situation in which he does not have to take account of other people's attitudes. Whatever he wants he can buy. Whatever he needs he can get, and he is not dependent upon anyone else at all. But of course this is a wholly illusory assumption. In fact, no one in modern society in independent. The fact that a man may be able to buy what he wants does not make him independent. It is still necessary for someone to make his clothes, to grow and process his food, to build his house, to manufacture his car, to print his newspaper, and so on. The fact that he can pay for these things does not make him less dependent upon his fellow men for the provision of them. It is, I think, often evident that the better off people become, the more they think they are independent. One interesting illustration of this is the way in which, as people become better off they live in bigger houses and therefore further away from their neighbour. It is notoriously true that in modern housing estates, especially those which are supposed to be what is called 'of a higher class', that is, occupied by a higher income group, the element of neighbourliness and mutual help is often remarkably small. Therefore the Christian contribution in the light of this tendency must surely be a continual reiteration of the truth that no one lives to himself and no one dies to himself. Against the tendencies of fragmentation and individualization of modern society, the Christian must continually emphasize our corporate responsibility and our need to think in all matters concerning human behaviour, not only of our own convenience, or of our own welfare, but also of the convenience and welfare and the good of society as a whole.

The second principle which emerges from Paul's discussion is the centrality of Christ in Christian morality. It is remarkable that throughout this passage Paul keeps on referring to 'Master' or 'the Lord' or to 'Christ'. He clearly thinks that this concept of the Lord is the determinative factor in the decisions to which he is referring. For instance, 'He who observes the day observes it in honour of the Lord; he also who eats, eats in honour of the Lord.' And, 'I know and am persuaded in the Lord Jesus that nothing is unclean in itself.' Or again, 'Do not let what you eat cause the ruin of one for whom Christ died.' Or, 'He who thus serves Christ is acceptable to God and approved by men.'[1] In all these comments we see Paul referring to that which was, of course, the dominant concept of the early Church, namely that Christ is alive, that to live a Christian life is to live it in Christ, as Paul himself often puts it; and that far from being someone who lived a long time ago and is now dead, Christ is the present living Saviour and Lord known in

[1] Romans 14:6, 14f. (RSV).

the Church. This means that the standard which the Christian must apply is that of relating all his activity to this living Lord. Applying this standard means that in the end a man must give account of himself to the Lord, and no one else must presume to judge what the relationship is between a man and his God. It is true that man must not disregard his responsibilities to the community in which he lives, but in the end, as St Paul puts it, 'If we live, we live to the Lord, and if we die, we die to the Lord, so that whether we live or whether we die, we are the Lord's.'[1] It is noticeable that these words, which are commonly used only in the funeral service, do not particularly apply to the Christian belief about life after death. They are much more relevant to the question of life here and now. The standard of Christian morality is in the sight of God revealed in Jesus Christ. That is, in the presence of your living Lord, is what you are doing something that you are sure is commendable, or is it condemned by Christ? This is the Christian attitude.

It is, of course, not easily comprehended by those who have no understanding of what it means to live in Christ. This means that part of the responsibility of those who advance this particular view is to do all in their power to help people to understand what life in Christ is. But it is also necessary to notice that this is a far more effective way of dealing with day to day problems of human conduct than the alternative ideal of what is good for humanity. We all know that moral decisions often come upon us without any warning and they often are very much involved with our desires and emotions. While it is not always true that that which is in agreement with our desires is wrong, it is often so. How can we find an effective standard which is strong enough to withstand the pull and the attraction of that which we desire for the moment? The Humanist seems to me to be forced into the situation of saying that we must always act in the light of what we think is good for humanity. This is a very laudable standard, but I doubt whether it is really practicable or effective. We need something more than a vague and impersonal concept of humanity to guide us in the times of real moral tension and decision. For a Christian this is provided by the living relationship with Christ.

This living relationship is built up in thought and worship

[1] Romans 14:8.

and activity. It is for a Christian no empty phrase to speak of doing that which is well pleasing to the Lord. Admittedly we can easily persuade ourselves that something is or is not well pleasing to the Lord, and we continually have to check a tendency to assume that what we *want* to do is what is well pleasing to the Lord. But still this standard is a possible and practical one for people to adopt. The Christian standard is 'live according to the light we have in Christ'. It is also good to remember, as St Paul says, that what we do must never injure one for whom Christ died. This is an extension of the claim and idea of life in Christ. For life in Christ is not really limited to those who openly recognize Christ as Lord and Saviour, but is in a real sense applicable to all mankind, since all men are men for whom Christ died. There is in this relationship with Christ a workable standard of Christian behaviour. It depends, as I say, upon the living relationship which a person has with his Lord, but this is a possible way of dealing with the everyday problems of morality with which we are all concerned.

It may be argued in answer to the assertions of the preceding paragraph that the Humanist is not in fact forced to depend upon a vague concept of humanity, for he has the principle of love to guide him. Act in love and you cannot go wrong, seems to be one of the very valuable insights that Humanists have into moral decisions. It is no part of a Christian's responsibility to argue against this. I am sure that we ought not to despise human love and we ought not to imply that the idea of acting in love is quite impracticable because human love is so unreliable a guide to our actions. But I think we do have to admit that there are certain limitations and defects in human love which must be recognized if we are to make acting in love a satisfactory basis for morality. Human love can be a very selfish attitude; it can be narrow and restricted.

To put the matter in parallel to the Christian standard outlined by Paul in I Corinthians 13, human love does sometimes end, it is sometimes arrogant, it is not always patient and kind; human love indeed is characteristically jealous, so much so that in the absence of jealousy many people wonder whether love is present at all. And it is certainly true that human love does often insist upon its own way and it does seek its own. Now the alternative to this is not to despise human love, but to lift it on to a higher plane through the standard and guide and example of Christ. By all means let us admit that it is a Christian view to act in love and to let love be our guide. This, I think, should be said without any hesitation or condition. What does need to be said also is that if we are to act in love in its fullest and most meaningful sense, we shall need a guide beyond our own impulses and the standards of our contemporaries. This guide for a Christian is found in the love of Christ. Quite simply, in him we see love embodied; for a Christian love is not truly known until we see it in Christ. This is surely what the first letter of John means when it says 'we love because he first loved us'. We see in Christ a way of love which is beyond our common experience and yet all the time appeals to us as the truly satisfactory way of love. Christ was the supreme embodiment of the love which did not seek its own, which was loyal, and consistent, and self-denying. This living embodiment of love which we have is the Christian's way of giving meaning and content to the principle 'act in love'.

We cannot do better than use the words of I Corinthians 13 to sum up what is the Christian way of living in love. 'Love is patient; love is kind and envies no one. Love is never boastful, nor conceited, nor rude; never selfish, not quick to take offence. Love keeps no score of wrongs; does not gloat over other men's sins, but delights in the truth. There is nothing love cannot face; there is no limit to its faith, its hope and its endurance' (NEB). Such a way of life is relevant to our present situation and applicable not only to personal responsibilities, but in a wider sphere. It needs continual responsible action on the part of those who follow this way to apply it in every new situation as it comes along.

As we turn to the specific questions which arise in the school situation, there are several aspects which require comment. In making these comments I am deliberately trying to avoid making dogmatic pronouncements or suggesting that we replace one legalism with another. I hope that I have made it clear in this book that I think that education is an invitation to an exciting adventure of ideas; it is a quest for a deeper understanding undertaken by teachers and pupils together. In no sense, so it seems to me, is it suitable for the teacher to lay down the law or provide easy answers to difficult and complicated problems, especially as children come to the age when they must make their own decisions about their own situations.

The first particular issue to which I wish to draw attention is the importance of the moral content of religious education. There are some who argue that moral education ought to replace religious education entirely. They can surely hardly have thought of the immense difficulties and problems of the basis for this kind of purely moral teaching. Compared with the admitted differences of views regarding various religious attitudes, the differences of moral views would be quite staggering. Surely the situation demands that for the full development of children an awareness has to be given of that aspect of life which to many people is its secret and its crown, namely the supernatural. On the other hand, teachers of R.E. do need to be aware of the danger of making the whole exercise too intellectual. If R.E. only deals with ideas and theories it is not likely to command much respect or enthusiasm on the part of most people, whose attitude is practical and non-metaphysical. R.E., in my view, should certainly be continually related to moral responsibilities and should uncover moral issues. Perhaps one of the chief contributions of R.E. in this connection is to give an opportunity for asking the relevant questions about traditional views of morality. The function of the teacher, especially of senior classes, is to raise the questions rather than give dogmatic answers to them. Why be good? What is 'the good'? Is 'the good' possible? Or is it an impracticable ideal? These are the sort of questions which young people need to be encouraged to ask and to which they have to find their own answers.

Another aspect of this matter which needs some comment is the criticism that Christian ethics are 'infantile'. This is the view of some leading philosophers and humanists who argue that the whole basis of Christian morality is childish dependence upon the authoritarian dictates of a person called 'God'. They argue that the practice and teaching of religion encourage an unnecessary and undeveloped dependence upon this supernatural figure, which dependence is often a transference of that previously directed at teachers and parents. As a child grows up he should be able more and more to stand on his own feet and to make his own decisions. Indeed, one of the objects of good education is to make a person able to stand on his own feet and live his life in its full extent according to his own wishes. But, say these exponents, Christian morality, by its infantile nature, is inimical to this particular aim. Christians will always be encouraged to a false dependence upon God or upon some other father figure, leading to a stunted development of their own moral sense. This criticism surely arises out of an over-legalistic view of morality which, admittedly, has often been advanced by Christian teachers in the past. I suggest that the force of this argument is largely vitiated when account is taken of the more open and flexible view of Christian morality which I have been endeavouring to expound. There are larger questions lying beneath this particular attitude connected with the whole relationship between religion and dependence, but these are questions which do not particularly or only arise with regard to problems of morality.

The third point that I think ought to be recognized is that there is an element of rebellion against secure mediocrity which is typical and natural to the young and which ought not to be discouraged. One of the most depressing features of so-called civilization is lower middle class suburbanity. This often degenerates into respectability made into a religion. It is a way of life which seems to be considerably reinforced by modern mass media which encourage conformity to accepted and general standards. Some of the protest hymns and songs which young people write and sing reflect their rebellion against this dull uniformity, this acceptance of the standard by which everybody else lives. Rebellion can, of course, be a very unpleasant and inconvenient thing. We have recently seen some rather disturbing examples of the destruction and waste of time and effort which accompany organized rebellion by the young against educational systems, economic attitudes and political decisions. But we should be very misguided as teachers if we thought these protests were wholly to be condemned. They are an expression of one of the most precious attitudes which belong to youth, namely, the attitude of rebellion and criticism. Surely the way to deal with this particular situation is not to try to impose harsher standards of discipline and rigorous rules of morality but rather to encourage young people to think out more deeply the implications of their rebellion and their criticisms. Only by this continual searching and questioning can anyone arrive at a deeper understanding of his own responsibilities. One of the curses of middle age is that we become more and more concerned to maintain the *status quo* and to think that the standards we have accepted and have tried to live by are the only standards which can ever be of any use to anyone.

One of the releasing and formative aspects of our modern society is that in many ways people are now able to choose freely what kind of life they live. I have said several times in this book that in my view this is a wholly good thing. Whatever problems this new freedom raises, it must be recognized as a great advance in human welfare that men are able to choose for themselves the manner of life they live. My closing comment on this ethical situation is on this line. Perhaps the greatest contribution that the older generation can make to the younger generation is to demonstrate the satisfactory nature of their way of life, not so much by words as by deeds. We do have the responsibility as teachers of making it quite clear to our pupils that it is *their* responsibility to choose what sort of life they live. They are now, within quite broad limits, able to decide freely what sort of persons they are going to be. You can be what you want to be, is something that is more true today than it ever has been in the past. And this, I repeat, is a good thing. Perhaps the most important aspect of moral teaching, therefore, is to show what in fact certain ways of life involve. We cannot hope that children will ignore the living example that we give them. We have a terrifying responsibility as teachers of young children who will accept almost anything we say far more readily than they accept what is said or done by their parents. This does not mean that we have to be plaster saints in order to be good teachers, but it does mean that we have continually to be showing our pupils what are the possibilities of human life opening up before them. In the end they have to decide what they want to be, but the responsibility is ours to make sure that they do know what they are deciding and that they do see in us a worth-while manner of life. The rest we have to leave to the common sense and good judgement of children as they grow up; and to the intrinsic value and attraction of the good life.

Index